the formative years

DOROTHY A. DIXON, Ph.D.

Published by Twenty-Third
Publications
West Mystic, Connecticut 06388

Library of Congress Catalog Number: 77-002106

Printed in the United States of America by Abbey Press, St. Meinrad, Indiana.

Cover, art, design, and layout by Bette S. Baker

Production management: Ed Curley
Editorial assistance: Elizabeth Grubb

To
Dorothea Gray Pflug, L.H.D.,
gentle spirit,
longtime laborer in the vineyards of early childhood

Table of Contents

Acknowledgements
Introduction
Chapter One: Fostering Intellectual Development 1
Chapter Two: Enabling Social-emotional Growth 13
Chapter Three: Nurturing Spiritual Growth 29
Chapter Four: Promoting Physical Development 45
Appendix 57
Bibliography 63

Acknowledgements

Over the years at Eden Laboratory School in Webster Groves, Missouri there has been a procession of little people coming into the classrooms each weekday morning at about nine o'clock. They come bringing "treasures" such as rocks, pieces of bark from trees, or "Matchbox" cars. They come with hugs and kisses and smiles, frowns, or comments such as "You know what? It's almost about to rain and I have a new umbrella in the car!" They come fully alive, and their zest for life is contageous. It is to them that I owe much inspiration for this book.

There are teachers at the school who are models of creativity, sensitivity, and professional skills. To them I owe much gratitude, because of the learning experiences they carry out which I describe in this book. Particularly, in the year in which this book is written, I have appreciated witnessing the teaching skills of Judith Lane, Dorrine McClelland, Ann Schroer, Jocelyn Secker-Walker, Jane Shea, Linda Spratte, Frances Smith, and Janet Thomas.

My secretary, Mary Beth McDonald has been helpful in typing some manuscripts, and Jan Virbikis, a student from Eden Seminary, has been helpful also in typing chapters. Tom Norwalk of Eden Seminary helped by taking some of the photographs for a related filmstrip program. To many others who participate in the ongoing program of the school, I send thanks and acknowledgements. The parents of the children enrolled at the school are an integral part of the program and are a constant source of inspiration.

World-famous authors such as Dr. Jean Piaget and Dr. Lawrence Kohlberg are progenitors for the thoughts and rationale behind this book. Because I have drawn on a wide variety of sources, I consider this approach to be eclectic, and therefore in the final analysis I must assume responsibility for all that is said in *The Formative Years.* But the book is a composite of thoughts and ideas which I am grateful to have received and to be able to share with you, the readers, who will extend human development by working with many persons in their formative years.

Introduction

Working with children in their formative preschool years is engaging in human development at its most basic level. At a time when the child is acquiring lasting attitudes and half the knowledge of a lifetime, the environment we plan is of utmost importance. Here we are, ready to share a portion of our lives with these little emerging persons. How can we enhance the quality of this time shared together? It is the purpose of this book to help us delve together into some answers to this vital question.

In a way, it is frightening to think of the privilege that is entrusted to us when we work with preschoolers. If we are parents, we are the most important teachers our children will ever have. If we are classroom teachers, we are called to muster all the skill, tenderness, and creativity we can possibly put forth. Some persons mistakenly think that nurturing preschoolers is not as serious as teaching at higher age levels. A volunteer once said to us, "I don't know anything about teaching, so put me with the three-year-olds." On the contrary, preschool teaching probably requires more skill, sensitivity, and understanding than teaching at any other age level.

This is not to say that every happening will make or break a child. Indeed, we all have days when we wonder: "Why didn't I handle that situation better?" But our very earnestness to continually improve our relatedness to children is an expression of a long-term caring that will be communicated at deeper levels. A parent or teacher who maintains a consistent relationship of caring and sensitive nurture is making an impact of permanent value in human development. Furthermore, it is in a caring and trustworthy environment that each person's faith acquires its foundation for life.

Then there are the rewarding times. They happen when Billy hugs you around the knees (that's as high as he can reach) and hands you a gift of a small bit of paper with three scribbles on it. They happen when Sally smiles her endearing smile and exclaims, "You know what? Nursery school is the funnest place I know!" Such heartwarming responses let us know that the children are off to a good start in life and that they can approach learning with joy and persons with love.

What kind of learning environment will elicit these kinds of responses? There are many good learning environments for preschool children in homes, day care centers, and nursery schools, and for each wholesome place, we rejoice. Each home and each classroom has its own unique personality, just as each individual is different.

We would not want to stereotype a place, and to say that one must be exactly the same as others. What we do wish to share in this book are some insights from one program which has nurtured little people over a number of years, and to invite you, our readers, to incorporate into your own environment whatever suggestions here that you think would be helpful.

Educating the Whole Child

At Eden Laboratory School, we try to balance the curriculum to include growth ingredients for all facets of learning: intellectual, social-emotional, physical and spiritual. From time to time we double-check to make certain each component is receiving its share of attention. For the purpose of analysis, we can separate these components, and discuss them one at a time. But we know that in actuality, they all grow together in the individual child, and that many learning experiences which we plan aid in all facets of development. For instance, the planting of seeds nurtures the intellect as it teaches biology. It is social, as children plan together. It is physical as the muscles go to work digging up the earth. And it is spiritual as the wonder of God's plan for growing things unfolds.

In this book, we will discuss the growth components separately, in order to bring out the many possibilities there are for each. But all the while we know that they are all a part of one growing process, working together in the life of each whole child.

Just as we make long range plans, we also plan for each individual day's activities. We value the daily lesson plans, as assurance that the child's activities are balanced, in the same way one might plan menus for balanced meals. But we do not stick slavishly to the daily lesson plans. One March day we had planned to make kites with the children. But early in the morning we were greeted by the sound of a rat-a-tat-tat outside our classroom windows. We looked to discover that a crew of sanitary engineers was digging up a sizeable portion of the street to put in a new sewer. The kites had to wait for another day as we gathered the children to go outside to watch the men in hard hats with their jack hammers.

Priority is always given to the child's need for discussion. When Danny comes in with news of a new baby in his family, or Susie brings her pet turtle to school, the lesson plan bends to the "ripe" topic for discussion. The combination of planning and flexibility is thus the clue to a really effective learning environment.

Creativity, Not Chaos

The school which we mention in this book could appropriately be described as having an "open classroom" or a "learning center" approach. This arrangement consists of many interest centers around the room. On a given day for instance, there would be a table for fingerpainting, a table with a cut-and-paste activity, a table with a learning game on it, and also the standard areas of block corner, housekeeping corner, paint easel, woodwork bench, and water table.

Each child enters the room, is greeted by the teacher, and then gets busy at the area of his or her choice. He or she is joined by others who have chosen that area. But as they feel a sense of completion in one spot, the children, one at a time, move on to other areas. The teachers are available for conversation, or assistance wherever requested. The child is thus allowed to exercise his growing skills in decision making, as to which activity he will pursue that day. By active involvement, the child begins to develop many concepts of shape, size, color, texture, sound, taste, and smell, in this multisensory environment. (One favorite tabletop activity is cooking—and for this, one teacher will stay at the table during the entire length of the activity.)

It takes a minimum of two teachers for this kind of classroom arrangement. One teacher may be involved in one specific activity while the other "floats" around the room to help as needed in the areas where children can usually work independently. The number of children in one classroom can range from 18 in the three-year-old room to 21 in the room of fours and fives. With volunteer help, the number of adults in a classroom may grow to three or four, so that more individual attention can be given.

It is true that there are some children who at age three or four cannot cope with so many interesting activities. Occasionally there will be a child who is bewildered by the number of choices. Sometimes one teacher will need to guide that one child from activity to activity, giving a suggestion of only two choices at a time, and carefully structuring the transition from one area to another. Occasionally, a child really needs to be transferred to a school that has a more rigidly structured curriculum. But for most children, the freedom within limits of this "learning center" approach is rich with opportunity for growth and development.

The classroom we describe is one that allows much room for creativity. There are many acceptable ways for the children to use the learning media. Patterns are seldom used, so that the child creates from his or her own inner aesthetic sensitivity, and no two creations appear alike. But it is not a permissive environment. The child knows that each medium has an area, and that it does not go beyond that limit. The blocks do not go into the paint area. The paintbrushes paint on the easel, not on any other surface. Fingerpainting may be done directly on the table top, because if it is used with detergent it wipes clean at the end of the period. But fingerpaint does not go off the table.

Children who are allowed this kind of freedom have their growing needs so satisfied that they seldom feel a need or urge to abuse the privileges. There is a minimum of disciplining because the children are absorbed in using their energies creatively. The room has a purposeful patter of noise, but it is not boisterous.

This is the beautiful balance between freedom and limits. There is much freedom to choose and do. But there is not freedom to abuse the environment or the people, and the children quickly learn the expectations of the room. This is the art of arrangement with the deep inner needs of the child in mind. If a wood sculptor carves with the grain of the wood he not only comes forth with an organically beautiful masterpiece, but he also is going the most effortless way. There is a sense in which the teacher is like that woodcarver. She is planning with the needs of the children in mind, and in time it becomes relatively effortless because there is not the struggle to go against the grain of the learner.

We see, then, that the classroom and the home need both order and freedom—both opportunities and limits. The child who is free within known limits is the child in the truly creative learning environment. The teacher, too, has limits. There are limits to how many choices should be offered in a given day. Some experiences need to be saved for a less busy time.

The balance of activity between quiet times and noisy times, between small-muscle tasks and large-muscle tasks, between listening and talking, between creative play time and group discussion time—this is the kind of balance a wholesome learning environment requires.

Why Preschool Education?

Some might ask why children need to be brought together for this kind of free-flowing experience. What is the value of constructing such an opportunity? Certainly our grandparents did not have nursery or preschool education, and they grew to be precious individuals.

But life is infinitely more complex than in grandmother's day. And not as much of a "slice of life" is available in the present home situation. Grandmother grew up where there were cows to milk, and churns for making butter. She had a garden in the yard and vegetables were grown and brought into the house to be cooked and canned. There was a small-town community where one could see almost all the processes of life going on, right in the neighborhood. Today life is so specialized that a small child can hardly be exposed to what life is all about unless a special learning environment is created. The home, the day care center, and the nursery school can offer exposure to many of life's processes.

Preschool education does not need to be highly structured, in fact, it is at its best when it is more informal than formal. The more closely a school or daycare center resembles a home, the better the small child can adapt to it, "feel more at home" and learn. But within this informal home-like atmosphere, small minds expand and character grows, and the awe and wonder of the universe have memorable expression. Yes, preschool education has its own characteristics. It requires planning and sensitivity. But it adds up to an opportunity for small children to experience life in its fullness, in a society that does not naturally lend itself to this kind of exposure. Often we are given evidence of how much the effort is effective in child development.

Once I told the children at group time about my great grandmother who was a Cherokee Indian. Her name was Granny Green, or at least that was what we called her. I told of how she lived in a place called "Ball Ground" Georgia, because there was a ball ground there and the tribes would play a game to settle a dispute. They let the winning team have their wishes in the dispute so that there was a settlement without war. At the time I wondered how much the children would remember from this unit on American Indians.

Several months later, as I sat on the rug for a different group time, four-year-old Katherine came up to me and crawled in my lap, put her arms around my neck and whispered "You know, I still am remembering about your Granny Green." This "feedback" was worth years of effort, for from it I realized that children often absorb more than we realize when we plan to expose them to a wide sweep of life.

Out of this kind of wide-ranged exposure to the wonder and beauty of life, a child develops the foundation for faith. The whole religious approach to life flourishes on this kind of faith basis, where children have learned to love and to trust in others, in themselves, and in God, the creator and sustainer of all the wonders and marvels that constantly surround us.

Dorothy Arnett Dixon was Director of Eden Laboratory School from 1971-1977. During this time she composed The Formative Years preschool program, including filmstrips. She is now Assistant Professor of Education at the University of Missouri—St. Louis.

Other books by Dr. Dixon are *Growth In Love* (the predecessor of this program), *World Religions for the Classroom* (a complete curriculum course), and *World Religions* (the concise paperback version of the earlier curriculum).

Chapter One

Fostering Intellectual Development

The Swiss psychologist, Dr. Jean Piaget, has given us some important clues to how a child learns. Probably the most important point he has made is that a small child does not learn by being told. Rather, the small child learns by *doing*—by "playing" with many objects, arranging and rearranging them until he has interiorized the experience or "assimilated" knowledge from his environment. Since the Piaget theories ,are the background for a good preschool cognitive curriculum, we share them with you in this chapter.

How Learning Occurs

The story is told that when the late Dr. Maria Montessori visited an institution for retarded children, it was reported to her that these children would get down from the dinner table and "go after" the crumbs on the floor. Dr. Montessori investigated the situation and found that the children were not at all hungry after their meal. They did not *eat* the crumbs under the table. But they played with the crumbs out of an innate need to experiment with objects. In their classrooms there were no manipulative materials, for the children were expected to learn by being told. Dr. Montessori then proceeded to bring into the retarded children's classrooms many objects such as buttons and ribbons for these children to sort and count and arrange. She found that making this kind of change in the curriculum advanced the learning level of the children considerably. In fact, many of the children learned enough to be graduated from this kind of special school into a regular environment. The problem had been that the curriculum was so geared to paper and books, to words and commands, that the children were actually "hungry" for something with which to play, even to the point of going for the crumbs under the table *(Standing, 1957 pp. 9-10).*

Thus we have learned that the intellectual development of the small child is dependent upon his opportunity to touch and "tinker" with a wide variety of objects. As he does this, he assimilates impressions into his mind. Only by "assimilating" or "drinking in" a stimulating environment can a child get a knowledge of what the world is all about. After a child "assimilates" many impressions, he begins to put like appearances together in his mind. He gradually begins to see that some objects are red, some green, and that some are round and some are square. He may even be figuring out that some things are large, some small, and that the large item may appear small when put beside something even larger. This is what Dr. Piaget calls "accommodation" which means sorting out impressions and putting thoughts into mental categories or concepts. Here is how learning takes place.

All of learning, then, takes place through these two processes of assimilation and accommodation, according to Dr. Piaget. We *assimilate* as we encounter something new in the environment—something that we see, hear, taste, touch, or smell,—and bring it into our mental storage house of impressions. We *accommodate* as we relate the new impression to what else we have assimilated in the past. Thus learning is like furnishing a house, if we compare the brain to a home. Assimilation can be compared to bringing furniture into the house. Accommodation can be compared to rearranging the furniture to make room for the new piece, and to make order or meaning out of the whole arrangement.

A child who is not exposed to many stimulating items or persons in his environment may not be assimilating very much. This is a deprived child who may appear to be dull, but is actually under-exposed to the variety of shapes, sizes, colors, textures, smells and sounds that life has to offer. But there is a point at which a child may be "overexposed." If too many conflicting sounds or sights are coming into the experience range of a child all at the same time, this is like bringing in furniture faster than a person could rearrange it to make sense out of it. Thus we see the need for the exposure to be paced to allow enough absorption time. The balance of assimilation and accommodation that goes on in each child's mind is called equilibrium. All of learning, then, according to Dr. Piaget, is brought about by assimilation, accommodation, and equilibrium.

Stages of Learning

At different stages of growth, children have different outlooks on life. At different ages and stages, children

see the world differently. The viewpoint of a child is quite different from that of an adult, and even different from that of children of different stages of development. It is helpful to know where the child in your family, daycare center, or classroom is in his stage of development. Then you can plan so that he can move on from that stage to the next.

Sensorimotor Period:

The infant is described as being in the sensorimotor period because he learns only by *sensing* (feeling, tasting) and acting upon *(motor)* his immediate environment. When an object touches his lips, he tastes or sucks it, and when something is within reach, he grasps it. Thus by using ready-made reflexes, the infant explores and learns. But during this whole period, that lasts from birth to 18 months or two years, learning is limited to what can be immediately seen, heard, tasted, smelled or touched.

The infant does not reason, but takes all appearances at face value. Whatever he sees he believes, but whatever he does not see does not exist, in his thinking. In this sensorimotor period, at first there is no idea of object permanence. The infant believes that he is all that matters—in fact he does not even realize that he is separate from his environment at first. He merely feels that he is all the world and that all around him is an extension of himself. Gradually he comes to see that he is separate from his environment. But when he does not see mother, he has no idea that she exists out of his sight. So his first world view is "I am the world" and his second world view is "things are separate from me, and they appear and disappear like magic." About eight months of age, however, the infant begins to get a slight notion that things might exist even when out of sight. Dr. Piaget proved this point with his own baby, Laurent. When the baby was six months old and Dr. Piaget held his watch before the baby's eyes, Laurent gazed with glee at the watch, but did not try to reach it when it was taken from view. But at eight months, the baby saw the watch, and saw his father's large hand come between the watch and his own view. Laurent then reached up, pushed the hand away, and gazed with delight at the watch. So Dr. Piaget knew that Laurent was finally beginning to reason that the watch was there even when the hand kept him from seeing it. *(Phillips 1969, p. 26).*

When Laurent was nine months old, his father, Dr. Piaget, placed his watch under two different coverlets. Laurent would lift up the first to find the watch, but would not lift up the second, even though he had seen his father place the watch under it. Evidently the baby was not enough convinced that the watch existed out of sight to pursue it in a second place. *(Ibid. p. 28).*

But when Laurent was 11 months old, and his father placed the watch alternately under two different pillows, the baby would look under both pillows until he found it. *(Ibid. p. 32).* We see from these examples a growing realization of the permanancy of objects.

Dr. Piaget also points out a growing ability at reasoning. His daughter Jacqueline, at age 14 months, tried to bring a stick into a playpen. The stick was horizontal. By trial and error she learned to bring it in vertically, parallel to the slats. Later, she quickly maneuvered the stick vertically, showing how learning is derived from the manipulation of objects. *(Ibid. p. 34).*

Thus, during the sensorimotor period of infancy, the baby has progressed from a totally egocentric view of life to a slight awareness of others, and a growing realization that things exist even when out of sight.

After two years of age, a child has enough use of language to be able to think in words or symbols, so the learning process is accelerated. But there still remains the lingering task of reinforcing the view that things exist when out of sight. Growth is never steady. A child will learn much about the permanancy of objects, yet will still have times of wondering if things really exist when out of sight. Preschool children begin their third year with some language and some notion of the permanency of objects, but the task of consolidating these learnings is still at hand.

Preoperational Period:

This period of life that spans the preschool years is called by Dr. Piaget, "preoperational." The "pre" means "before," and the "operational" means being able to think and act with a whole view of the situation. An "operational" person has a background and general understanding for the whole scene, so that each part is seen as a detail in a complete picture. The preoperational child sees only the details, without an understanding of the relationships among the details.

We have a picture of "Woodlands" at our preschool. As adults we see the whole picture, which includes tall trees whose branches meet overhead, and a pathway leading through ferns and fallen leaves. In the lower right corner of the picture, there is a small spider in a web. What do you think the preschool children say about the picture? "It's a spider" they invariably remark, because they notice the detail rather than the whole of the picture. The small child "centers" on details rather than wholes. He is "preoperational."

There are several other characteristics of the preoperational child, which we will discuss as we share ways in which we can edge the child on to more mature levels. Meanwhile, let us glimpse the further stages of development that will grow after preoperational years, provided the environment offers enough oppor-

tunity for the child's active involvement with a number of objects and persons.

Concrete Operations Period:

During the early elementary years, the child will go through the period of "concrete operations." This period is the time when the child can see life in whole views—can understand concepts of size and shape and color but only in terms of concrete objects that he can behold with the five senses. During that period he consolidates his growing awareness of object permanence, and the permanency of *area,* quantity, weight, volume, time, etc. But only in terms of tangible objects.

Formal Operations Period:

At about 11 years of age, the child gains the final stage of intellectual growth when he can picture in his mind all of reality. He can think in abstract as well as concrete terms, he can develop hypotheses of what might be, and test fact and contrary-to-fact propositions. He can think in terms of ideas as well as objects.

This, then is the sweep of the learning process, from the infantile sensorimotor period to preschool preoperational period, to early elementary concrete operations, to formal operations, which come in late childhood or adolescence.

Five Tasks for Preschool Learning

Let's look now at some of the learning needs of preschoolers, so we can have these in mind as we consider our own learning environment.

1. Decentering.

One of the main tasks for preschoolers is the task of decentering. We have spoken already of how a small child notices many details, but seldom sees a whole pattern. This characteristic of all preschoolers is called "centration" because it has to do with their concentrating on bits and pieces rather than on wholes. Our task is to edge the child along toward the ability to decenter on parts and perceive the whole. But it takes many experiences and several years, before the child begins to see the whole of which many things are parts. This is why preschool puzzles are important, because they teach part-whole relationships. There are other learning games designed for this need which we use at our school. One is called "What's Going Through the Tunnel?" This game shows part of a firetruck, but the rest is out of sight. When the page is opened, the whole firetruck is seen, inside the tunnel. Games such as these can be made from magazine pictures. But practice in seeing that bits can be part of a larger whole is one special intellectual need of the preschool child.

2. Overcoming egotism.

Even as we are hard at work on

"decentering" tasks, there is also the task of enabling the child to see beyond his own viewpoint. It is inconceivable to him that others see life differently. For instance if a four-year-old is shown a picture of three mountains—one small, one middle-sized, and one large—in a row, he can identify the different sizes. But if we were to ask him how the three mountains would look if we were standing at a different angle, he could not identify the new pattern because it would necessitate taking another's point of view. Try this exercise on an older child—say age nine, and he will probably say that the mountains look like three mounds with the larger ones appearing behind the smaller—but that is an assertion that takes more understanding than a preschooler can muster. To the preschooler, life is only as it looks from his vantage point, and no other way.

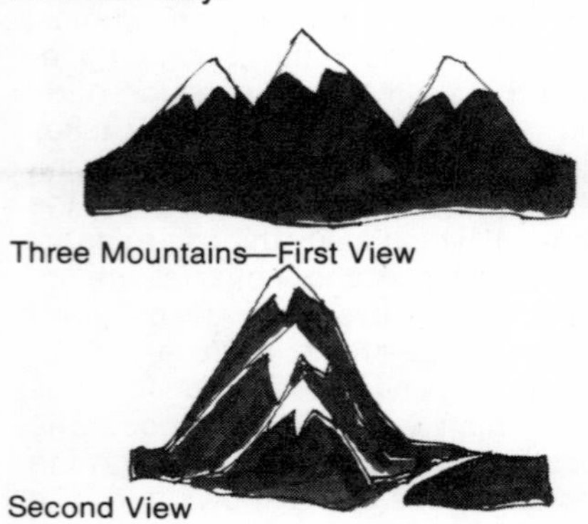

Three Mountains—First View

Second View

Fig. A

But we can help the preschooler grow beyond his "egocentrism." We can plan learning tasks that edge him along to a more mature awareness. For instance we can place an interesting block structure on a table. We can put four chairs around the table. We can have children describe what they see, each as he or she sits in a different chair. Then we can have the children rotate, changing seats so that they get a new "view" of the block structure. Then they can describe what they saw, discovering that it looks like what Susie said when sitting in the chair Susie first occupied, and it looks like what Billy said when sitting in the chair he first occupied. Games such as this help children to see that different views of the same objects vary. Children learn most by interacting with peers. When two children clash over a difference of opinion, eventually they discover that there are others who have views different from their own. Peer play is the best method of moving a child beyond preschool egocentrism.

3. Discovering transformations:

Another task is to enable the preschooler to discover the transformations that occur in properties. Preschoolers notice only the final outcome of a transformation, not the process by which it occurred. For instance, if there are two glasses of liquid, each containing an equal amount, the preschooler will agree that the amount is equal. But if you pour one glass of liquid into a differently shaped container—say a taller and thinner one—the child will say at the outcome that there is more liquid in the new container than in the remaining one. He judges by the fact that now the liquid registers higher than in the wider containers. He does not reason that none of the liquid was spilled, and that none has been added; therefore it must be the same amount. He judges by the outcome, rather than the process or transformation. (See Fig. B)

Another example of this characteristic is the experiment with two balls of clay. They should be equal. The child agrees they are equal in size. Then roll one ball out into a sausage shape. Ask the child if there is more, less, or the same amount of material in the ball that is rolled out. He will invariably tell you that there is more clay in the sausage shape, even though none was added or subtracted in the transformation process. (See Fig. C) But with years of manipulating clay and pouring liquid, gradually the preschooler will emerge into the next stage of knowledge in which he reasons that there is no difference in the matter unless some more is added or unless some is subtracted. Thus our task, with many materials, is to provide experience from which the preschooler gradually can learn to notice not only the appearance of an item, but also the transformation of *how it got* that way.

We are not so anxious to speed up the process of knowledge as thoroughly to ground the learners in experience, so that the knowledge is on solid foundations of understanding. Logical thinking will flourish in an environment that allows much interaction on the part of a child. The goal is not to speed the learning from stage to stage, but to *thoroughly* nurture the child through experiences that give much background for real wisdom growth. It has been said that "you can grow a squash in a summer, but it takes 20 years to grow an oak tree." In this analogy, the oak tree is the strong, lasting model, with the good long growing season. A child may learn to read at age three, but what is the benefit? His eye muscles may be unduly strained before readiness, and a late reader reads as well as an early reader. Instead of pushing reading, we prefer to have a school for *thinking* where logical thought is based on solid experience. Later, when reading comes along, it will have more meaning because of all the understanding that has been slowly accruing in the experienced mind!

4. Learning to think in reverse:

Closely akin to transformations is the concept of reversibility. It is impossible for a very small child to think in reverse. Only gradually, as the child is beyond his fifth birthday, can he realize that what goes forward can go backward, what goes up must come down, and what goes in may come out. Like a movie film that can be played forward and backward, an adult mind can think in two directions. But to the small child, the event is finished in one direction. With this characteristic in mind, we can understand why a preschooler cannot stand to lose a game. It is inconceivable to him to reason "if I lost, he won, so he has good feelings and perhaps next time he will lose and I will win." That kind of thinking requires

The liquid in the containers

Fig. B

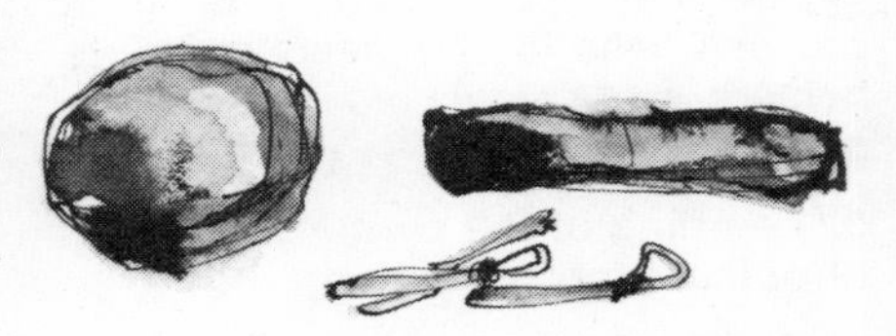

The two balls of clay

Fig. C

the maturity of reversible thinking. Thus win-lose games are a disaster in a preschool room. They are fun for early elementary children who can think in reverse, so we save our rules games for later.

Meanwhile, much experience such as nonwinner games can edge the preschooler along toward reversibility. "Go in and out the window" is a time-honored group game that gives experience in "in-out" reversing. Seesaws teach reversibility, especially if an adult rhythmically comments, "Now Johnny is up and Beth is down—now Beth is up and Johnny is down." Or throwing a ball and calling out, "It's up, it's down" can point the way to reversibility. Stories can help children empathize with others whose feelings are real—to edge the child along toward the goal of being able to see life from another's point of view. But if a mother says to a preschooler, "Please be quiet so I can sleep, I have a headache," it may be that the child will not be quiet very long. To the child, it is hard to understand that mother's head hurts when the child's head feels fine. This is not to say that preschoolers are not tender in sympathy—they can be beautifully responsive to others. When one child had a bumped lip at Eden Laboratory School, another child brought her a toy to "make her feel better." This was simple empathy. "She feels bad so I'll help her feel better." But thinking in reverse, like actively taking another's point of view, is still a growing need for the preschooler. As helpers, we can only plan to edge the growth along.

5. Learning of the permanency of objects (conservation):

The final task for the preschooler is to learn conservation. Remember how the child in infancy had no idea of the permanency of things? He thought that things just magically appear and disappear. The preschooler does have some notion of permanency—knowing that there can be things that exist even when out of sight. But that simple knowledge needs yet much expansion.

If two even rows, each containing eight checkers, are placed before a four-year-old, the child will agree that there are the same number of checkers in each row. But if one row is shortened, by pushing the checkers closer together (but removing none) the child will decide that there are less checkers in the shorter row. This is the reasoning of a little mind that has not yet learned that number stays the same regardless of the arrangement. So the task is to develop conservation of number in the child—the ability to see that the number cannot change merely by the rearrangement of the parts. Many opportunities to arrange and rearrange the checkers will eventually convince the child that the number stays the same. (See Fig. D)

Dr. Piaget once placed several eggs in egg cups. He asked a child if there were the same number of eggs as cups, and the child said "yes." Then he took the eggs out of the cups and put them in a bunch. The child then, looking at the longer row of cups, commented that there were more cups than eggs. Preschoolers judge by appearance, not logic. They think that things are as they appear to be, not as they logically must be. The practice of putting eggs in and out of cups, or checkers in rows will gradually edge the child along to developing the logic of conservation of numbers. (See Fig. E)

Then there is another task—to develop conservation of area. If there is a square with four blocks in it, and the

Row 1:

Row 2:

Are there more checkers in Row 1?

Fig. D

Are there more egg cups than eggs?

Fig. E

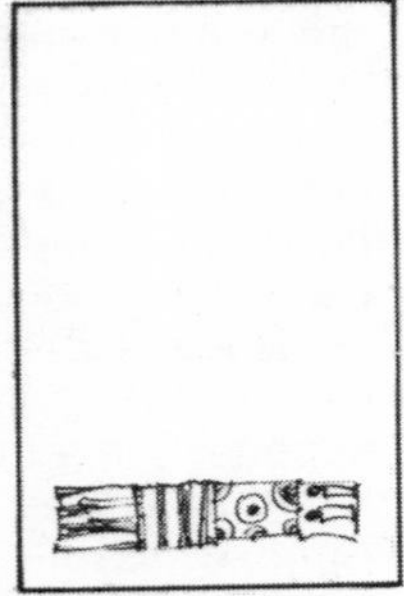

Which area has more free space?

Fig. F

child sees the area not covered by the blocks she will say there is more bare area when the blocks are side by side, than when scattered. It appears that way. But can it *be* that way? (See Fig. F) Repeated practice with simple games such as this will help the child to interiorize the logic of the conservation of area. Manipulating many objects is the growing opportunity that enables real logical thinking to develop. It need not be hurried. But it must be well-planned and varied, paced to offer enough but not too much intellectual stimulation each day.

The Learning Environment

Since the children learn by doing, our classrooms and homes need to abound in opportunities for experimentation with a variety of colors, shapes, sizes, and textures. Perhaps on one tabletop there will be construction paper shapes of triangles, squares, rectangles, circles, and hexagons. The children make collages by pasting these shapes on paper in

whatever order they find pleasing. By arranging and rearranging these colors and shapes, the children are interiorizing the concepts of shape and color. If the shapes are of varying sizes, the children are also absorbing concepts of "big, middle-sized, and little." Or there can be Fall leaves to sort and arrange. Boxes, bottles, spools, and all sorts of throwaway material can be used for making three-dimensional arrangements.

On the commercial market, there are a number of construction sets that are educational for children in a home, classroom, or day care center. Some of the favorites at Eden Laboratory School are: Bristle Blocks, Constructo Straws, Tinker Toys, Lincoln Logs, Chrystal Climbers, and Stacking Clowns. The value of such materials is in the child's chance to manipulate and fit together the many shapes and colors. There is no right or wrong in construction sets. The child is free to fit pieces together as he or she pleases. Blocks are among the most important equipment in the nursery school—especially the unit blocks of hard wood, the hollow blocks that are larger, and cardboard blocks that are lightweight. Stacking, arranging, and rearranging this equipment gives a child a strong sense of the relativity of size and special relationships. Creativity is encouraged by the child's freedom to manipulate materials many ways.

But we also need learning equipment that is more structured. Sets that go together only one correct way serve a special purpose. For instance, picture puzzles can be put together only one way. These are thus called "reconstruction" toys because when taken apart they are to be "reconstructed." Reconstruction materials teach order, in a "fun sort of way." Homemade reconstruction sets can

be games for seriation, or games for classification. For seriation, the task is to line up rods from the shortest to the longest. We can make the rods from dowel sticks, or from cardboard rolls, or from corrugated cardboard. The set will have lengths varying at regular intervals. Also for seriation we can have a stack of sandpaper pieces of varying coarseness. The task for the child is to line up the pieces from roughest to smoothest. In all seriation games, the task is to arrange the materials in an order. One resourceful teacher made some "listening cans" in which she put items such as rocks or sand. The child then had the fun of shaking each can and deciding which was loudest in the noise it made. Then the cans could be lined up from loudest to softest, in a task of seriation.

Other games that have only one right outcome are classification games. Here the task is to put like things together. Games such as this can be made with salvage containers

such as our row of cottage cheese containers, into which the children sort different colors of blocks; or an empty egg carton into which children sort matching buttons, or other items. But the task is to put like things together.

Many beneficial seriation and classification games are listed in the *Workjobs* book by Mary Baratta-Lorton. (See bibliography.)

Stringing beads is not only good coordination exercise, but can be a skill-producing task if the beads are to match a specified pattern. Children may put a red, a blue, and a yellow, followed by the same three colors in that order, over and over again. More complex patterns, involving beads of varying shapes as well as varying colors, can be made, with the children set to the task of matching them. Children at our school use the McGraw-Hill "Loose beads and lace" boxes with pattern cards to go with them, for this task.

Then there are games that can be played with the varying colors and shapes. Color and Shape Bingo, or lotto games with color and shapes are good if done *not* for competition, but for skill building. *Thinking is Child's Play* has a number of such games for three-year-olds. Preschoolers usually think that an item is either red or round but not both. Dr. Piaget once had a set of wooden beads, 18 brown and two white. He asked a preschooler if there were more brown beads, and the preschooler answered yes. But when he asked if there were more wooden beads, the answer was no, because it is difficult for a preschooler to think in terms of two attributes (color and substance) at one time. To play with sets of varying color and shapes edges growth along to the realization of the many attributes of each object.

In the same way that a preschooler has difficulty thinking of two attributes at a time, he also has difficulty thinking of two roles at a time. Imagine the surprise when a pupil from the school meets his teacher in the grocery store, with a baby in her arms. The preschooler will invariably remark, "You can't be a mommie, you're a *teacher.*" But the experience is good because it edges along the realization that we all play many roles in life simultaneously. Therefore we encourage our teachers to show children pictures of their own children, or to bring their children to class from time to time. (It is good for the teacher's children to see how "Mommie" looks in the role of teacher, too!)

Beyond concept formation, there is the whole realm of the animated world that can be exposed to children. The animal kingdom, the plant kingdom, all the varieties of people and customs on earth, the different occupations persons pursue—all are a vital part of a preschool program.

As the child visits places that abound in growing things, his world horizon expands. A trip to a farm, to a zoo, to a concert, to a hospital—all are delightful and highly instructive parts of a curriculum.

Just before Halloween, the children at Eden Laboratory School visited a pumpkin farm. They went into the fields, and were allowed to pick pumpkins and gourds right off of the vines. Imagine the mind-expansion that was going on that day! The variety of sizes of pumpkins was noted, the variety of colors on the gourds became a source of marvel, and the bumpy and smooth textures of the gourds were a delight for small fingers to sense. Then there was the observation of roots, stems, and leaves on the vines, and the unbelievable recognition that all this wonder grew from small seeds planted in the springtime.

Adventures such as these are actually growth-producing in all areas of development: They are intellectually stimulating; they are social interaction as friends roam fields together; they are physical exercise as little bodies haul large pumpkins to the wagons; and they are spiritual nurture of the child's intuitive relatedness to the Divine splendor and plan that permeates the created world.

In this chapter we have given attention to "How Learning Occurs," the "Stages of Learning," "Five tasks for Preschool Learning" and "The Learning Environment." It is our hope that more and more children can be exposed to a stimulating and creative environment in their formative years.

Chapter Two

Enabling Social-Emotional Growth

Rebecca and Catherine are in the "housekeeping corner," busily donning necklaces to go with their fancy long dresses and high-heeled shoes. They gaze with admiration at themselves in a long (unbreakable) mirror, and giggle together at the sights they behold. Totally unselfconscious, they try on garment after garment, visualizing themselves as grown ladies in spite of the fact that they are only four years old. Their projection of themselves into the future is a part of the healthy "stretch" of gender identification, and it can take place in a classroom during the creative play time when a myriad assortment of other activities are also taking place.

Sex Role and Gender Identification

A visitor for that day might ask, "But isn't this activity a way of stereotyping the girls in an era of a more liberated emphasis?" If the visitor remained to observe longer, however, he or she would notice how much is also done to teach that role expectation must be very open for both sexes. Open role expectation means that a person should be able to choose a career without feeling limited by being a girl or being a boy. Even the hobbies and life styles need to be free from old stereotypes that would limit the way life is to be led.

For instance, the visitor at Eden Laboratory School would notice that the small figures for playing "Community Helpers" are in double sets so that there is a doll dressed as a woman doctor and another to represent a man as a doctor. For each profession and trade there is both a male and a female figure, to teach that either sex can pursue each career. The teaching pictures of professional persons also come in two's—male and female for each. In the play areas, boys and girls alike are invited regardless of whether it is a place to rock a doll or a place to nail together bits and pieces of wood.

It is not always easy to create an environment where the role expectations are open. Society still has residues of outmoded attitudes, and it is not unusual to hear boys in the block corner shun girls who want to play there. Skillful teachers and parents need to muster their best sensitivity to enable play to be more open. Sometimes children's books can help build the kind of attitudes that are wholesome—books like *A Doll for William* and *A Train for Jane* (See bibliography). Books like these can build for a future in which society recognizes the need for daddies to rock babies. For how many centuries have we cheated men of the joy of feeling really close to their own children? The child psychiatrist, Dr. Paul Painter, once made the statement that the tragedy of many homes is that so many fathers are "psychologically absent" from their children. The kind of play that we foster among children can contribute to a future where each child will have *two* nurturing parents.

Another need in a role-free atmosphere is the opportunity for all children, girls and boys alike, to express their emotions. For how many centuries have parents said to their small sons, "Little boys don't cry"? How many pent-up tears have men carried into their adult years when the real need was to shed them when the situations were ripe? One year at Eden Laboratory School there was a small boy who would not cry, even when hurt. Evidently he had been a victim of the outmoded "little boys don't cry" stereotype. Our concern was for the real feelings that were bottled up under the grim stoicism of that small boy. The teachers spoke often of how we need to cry when hurt, because crying helps us get rid of the hurt. One day the boy, working at the workbench, hit his thumb with the hammer accidentally, and he twisted his face in the grimace of pain. The teacher nearby commented quietly, "I know how much it hurts because I hit my thumb with a hammer a few days ago and I really cried."

The boy looked up with an almost "may I?" expression in his eyes, and suddenly let himself go in a flood of tears. The teacher took him in her arms, and held him as he sobbed, then together they went for ice to put on the injured thumb. The child cried for five or 10 minutes—long enough to release four years worth of pent-up emotions, and then went back to play with the brightness of expression of a man set free.

Another good way of opening the role expectations of boys and girls is to expose the children to persons who have pursued professions openly. Wherever there is a woman doctor or a woman dentist, let the children be introduced. A woman lawyer, or a woman mechanic would be wholesome persons for children to meet. Professional persons of different races also should be made available for conversation with children so that each child can identify with an adult who becomes a role model.

So we have explored the growing need to enable children to feel free to develop fully and freely and responsibly, regardless of whether they are girls or boys. This is what we mean by open role expectations. But there is still the underlying need for each person to establish his or her own gender identification. Gender identification is not open like role expectation. A basic need for each girl and boy is to recognize and accept with gladness the gender in which he or she was born.

Psychologists tell us that by the age of three a child must know that he or she is a girl or a boy. To accept one's own sexuality is as important as to be free in the role one will play in life. Sometimes in the move toward role freedom we may neglect the basic need for gender identification. One year at the nursery school there was a girl who looked so much like a boy that the children referred to her as "him." Her hair was cut very short, and most children at the school wear slacks or blue jeans, so it is easy to mistake the sex of a child. How could we establish proper gender identification without calling attention to the little girl and embarrassing her?

Skillfully, a classroom teacher devised a plan. Just after group time, when it was time for the children to go over to the table for snacks, this teacher called each child individually, by name and by sex, so that the children were each reinforced in gender identification, including the little girl who needed this reinforcement the most. Quietly, the teacher would say "Now if you are a boy and your name is Billy, you may go to the snack table." Billy would rise from the rug area and go to a table. Again: "Now if you are a girl, and your name is Susie, you may go to the snack table," and Susie would rise and go to the table. In this way no child was singled out yet all were identified as to name and sex, and it made a kind of fun game out of a most important task. Each day for a month this procedure was followed, after which there was no question as to the sex of the little girl with the short hair!

Thus we see that in social-emotional development a prime task is to enable each child to establish a wholesome gender identification. The two girls described earlier who were enjoying dressing up like ladies were really projecting their gender identification into the future. To do this they were identifying with an adult of their same sex. But those same girls are also learning that as ladies they will be free to pursue their own human development to the fullest, choosing whatever roles, vocations or avocations they earnestly desire in life.

Developing Self-esteem

Having established "who I am," the child needs further to explore "how do I feel about myself?" Unless a child can realize his or her own worth that child cannot recognize the worth of others. If a child devalues himself, he will project that self distaste on others. The ability to relate with joy to others, then, depends on the prior ability to value one's self. How can we, as parents and teachers, enhance the self-esteem in each child?

The first step begins with our own attitude toward each child. Children sense how adults feel about them, and they tend to echo those adult feelings. As we examine our own attitudes toward each child, we may find that we have many mixed feelings. It is possible that a child may have annoying patterns of behavior, but our calling as a parent or teacher is to see beyond the behavior to the value of the self. Then in this framework of love and respect, we can help the child overcome disruptive habits. Love grows for each child as association continues, and often it grows the most for the child who offers the most challenge!

Sometimes we find ourselves almost overwhelmed with delight in our relatedness to each child. Each child needs to know how much we value him or her. The psychologist Dr. Carl Rogers urges that all adults who work with children view them with "unconditional positive regard." It is only in this kind of emotional atmosphere that children really grow and thrive. In most cases children sense the way adults feel about them, The nonverbal expression of approval and acceptance is the art of skillful parenting and teaching. But words help, also.

Whenever a child is helpful or creates something aesthetically beautiful, our appreciative comments can give the necessary encouragement. We can comment honestly: "Paul, I really like the way you have cleaned the table top—it almost shines!" Or, "Karen, I noticed how quickly and evenly you stacked the blocks away!" Specific praise is the most valuable type, because it lets the child know that you really noticed, and are not just trying to be nice. For instance if a child has painted a picture at the easel, even if it is a most ordinary application of brush strokes, we can find something about it that catches our attention. Then honestly and descriptively we can say: "Larry, you know what I like most about your painting? I like the way the blue and the yellow overlap here to make this interesting green area." This comment is an example of what is called "descriptive praise" and it lets a child know you have really noticed his or her work.

Another step in building self esteem is the planning of activities at which each child can succeed. Sometimes individual planning is needed for certain children. For a child to complete a task with a sense of "I did it" is not only exciting but is basic to good social-emotional development. Success builds a positive self-regard, and this in turn enables children to relate with joy to peers and to adults. Occasionally, to give a child a challenge beyond past performance, we may plan a more difficult task. If it is successfully completed, the "aura of well being" is enhanced. But for a child who is secure and has already experienced much success in other endeavors, it will not be devastating to experience one failure.

One morning Joe attempted to build an igloo out of "Giant Tinker Toys." He got the dome completed,

but when he tried to set it on "walls," it came crashing down. Joe was heard to mutter under his breath, philosophically, "Oh well, back to the drawing board!" (Fortunately Giant Tinker Toys are hollow and light so that even an avalanche of them inflicts no bodily harm.) We are saying, then, that occasional failure in a general pattern of success is all right. But the larger point is that most activities need to be ones that will give a sense of success and accomplishment. Frustrating tasks, far beyond a child's ability, need to be avoided.

The chance to do things for himself is a vital need in a young child's life. When play time is over, the children themselves need to put the toys away. Parents and teachers can stand by to facilitate, or occasionally to work with the children, but basically the children need to exercise self-sufficiency to do their own tasks. In a classroom or a home where several children are involved, it is good to have general cleanup, with each person "pitching in" regardless of which area each child had used. Words such as, "We all enjoyed the room, so we all help in setting it straight" avoid the kind of argument that could ensue if each child cleaned only where he had played. Committees for cleaning various areas of the room can give organization to the process.

Group cleanup time is usually announced by a song such as:

> "It's time to put the toys away,
> The toys away, the toys away,
> It's time to put the toys away,
> So we can play another day."

Cleanup then becomes not a chore but a logical part of the play process. The group cleanup at the end of a creative play period involves all equipment that has been used by more than one child. If a child, during the group play, had taken a puzzle off the shelf and worked it, that child would have returned the puzzle already. But the value of the group cleanup is the fostering of a feeling of cooperation.

Competition for preschool children is not wholesome. It is very hurtful for a child to be compared to another child. A child can be motivated by seeing his work in comparison with his or her own past performance, but to motivate by comparing one child to another is to foster hurt feelings and even resentment.

An excellent way to bring a child's positive self-concept into focus is to engage in the process of making "All About Me" booklets. These booklets can be merely pages of paper stapled together, with a "cover" selected from the child's best artwork. Pages in the booklet could include: a hand print, a foot print, a "data" page listing height, weight, color of eyes, etc., and a page with a story about the child's family. These stories can be dictated to an adult who writes them up for the booklet. There can be a page listing the child's favorite foods, favorite animals, favorite places to visit, favorite colors, etc.

Another graphic way of building self-esteem is to make an outline of the child's body, on large brown wrapping paper, and then to cut out the shape and put it on the wall. Sometimes the children like to color the clothing on this "life sized paper doll" or to print their names on it. In this way each child can stand back and see his or her own figure. At the end of a year it is fun to measure to see how much the children have grown.

Whenever a child creates a pleasing work of art, the picture or art form needs to be recognized. This can be done by placing it on a wall at the nursery school or day care center, or by having the child take it home for display. Whatever a child brings home must be noticed, even if it is only a strip of paper to show that the child can now use scissors. Hopefully, the child's art will be his own work, not a "teacher-made" project. Therefore the importance is in the self-expression rather than in the finished product. Children's art should be valued for its own sake, and not judged by adult standards.

Thus we see valuable self-esteem growing in children from a sensing of the adults' "unconditional positive regard," from appropriate words of praise, from planning for success, from opportunities for self-sufficiency, from "All About Me" booklets, from life-sized silhouettes, and from the prominent displays of children's artwork. We move on, now, to other components of healthy social-emotional development.

Talking About Feelings

Children have many feelings, and they need a chance to talk about them. In our small-group times, we like to give children a chance to talk about happy times, sad times, angry times, or fearful times. There are many ways of leading into these subjects, and each adult finds his or her own way. The important need is that time be set aside at regular intervals for talking about feelings.

In a small group discussion recently, (involving one adult and six children), we talked of happy times we remembered spending with our families. It was interesting and encouraging to hear of the many special times the children could remember and describe the topic. Emily told of going to an amusement park with her family and riding the "log floats." Jennifer told of her family's trip to Disneyland. Christopher told of how the neighborhood where he lives blocked off one end of the street and had a "block party" for all the families that live there. Another child told of a camping trip and "playing in a ditch" with his brothers. Rebecca told of the time her family went to the beach, and that even though she was afraid of the waves, that she had fun playing on the sand. Andrew told of the wonderful day when his father took him to the zoo. The common element in each

story was the experience of happiness in the family group at a time of a special outing. It was really rewarding to hear the children discuss happy times with an obvious knowledge of the feeling they described. "Being happy," said one, "is when you just feel glad all over!"

With this same group, the next time we met to discuss feelings, the topic changed to the emotion of fear. It was just before Halloween, and we talked on "something I used to be afraid of that I don't fear any more." One child told of how he used to be afraid of Frankenstein. We discussed seeing this monster on television, and then we tried to decide whether he was really real. The children agreed, for the most part, that Frankenstein is "make believe," and that therefore we do not need to live in fear of him. One child, who had been listening to the conversation then expressed her own breakthrough: "You know what, I used to be afraid of ghosties, but really there's no such thing as ghosties!" Her remark set the tone for all that was to follow.

A small boy told of how he was going to be Batman for Halloween. We talked about how you can pretend to be anybody, but underneath your costume on Halloween it's really you. We agreed it's fun to pretend. But we also agreed that in reality "there's no such thing as a monster or a ghost or Batman." Separating fantasy from reality can be liberating for children. Then the imaginations can expand while the fear is minimized.

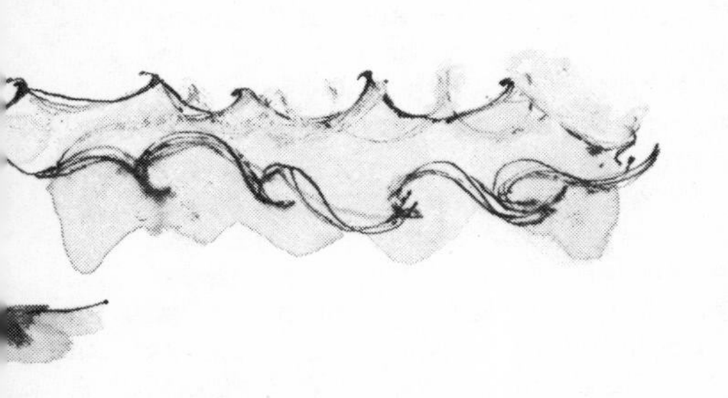

In order to sort out valid fears from the ones we no longer need, we talked about the times when it is really good to be afraid. We talked about crossing busy streets—when a little fear will instill caution—and about the sound of thunderstorms that drives us to seek shelter. This was a helpful discussion to counteract the notion that fear is a sign of weakness. Fear can be healthy if it is valid fear. But make-believe is fun and should not cause real fear in boys and girls who have learned to sort fantasy from reality.

Then there was the day when we talked of anger. Our topic was: "Something that really makes me mad is—." One boy told of how it makes him angry when his brother hits him. Another boy chimed in that he gets mad when the older boys will not let him play with them. A girl told of how somebody knocked her block house over, and she was mad because she had just got the house finished. Another child told of a sister taking a toy, without asking permission, and the angry feelings the incident caused. We tried to keep the conversation centered on "what" makes us angry—not on "who." But the value of the conversation was that we enabled the children to see that everybody gets angry at one time or another. Feelings need to be discussed so that we can view them objectively and understand that they are a normal part of life.

If we discuss feelings calmly in a group setting when there is no crisis at hand, we develop awareness and language skills that can be used in more turbulent times. Then when a crisis occurs, and one child is feeling the rage of anger, he has the ability to tell how he feels. Thus we build toward the use of words in conflict resolution.

To discuss the feeling of sadness, we used a smile face and a frown face on opposite sides of a yellow paper. We then discussed the way we sometimes feel happy and sometimes feel sad. Then we made a list of happy feelings and sad feelings, and the list read like this:

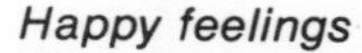

Happy feelings

"My mommie let me sleep with her"

"My mommie let me help her in the kitchen"

"My sister let me play with her doll house"

"My daddy read stories to me"

Sad feelings

"When I am all alone"

"When I dropped my ice cream cone"

"When our dog died"

"When I couldn't go swimming because I had a cold"

After our list was finished, we read together first the sad entries, then the happy ones, and concluded by saying "Sometimes we're sad and sometimes we're happy, and isn't that interesting?" This was a way of recognizing the full gamut of feelings in life.

Some parents and teachers like to use some of the Golden Press Books in the Menninger Foundation series that deal with these and other topics: *Sometimes I'm Jealous, Sometimes I'm Afraid, Sometimes I get Angry.* The books then lead into a discussion of the child's feelings. There are many other resources on the market for beginning a discussion of feelings. (See the bibliography for a few of these—watch advertisements for new materials coming on the market.)

Often a picture, cut from a magazine, will make a good discussion starter. The face in the picture may convey such a marked expression that the children can talk about what they see, and what they think is happening in the picture. Then they can talk about similar situations in their own lives. Thus from a picture, or a book, or an announced topic, the discussion of feelings takes place with a few children and an adult, and the results are healthy attitudes toward each person's own emotionality.

Resolving Conflicts

When we plan to meet the needs of children, there is a minimum of conflict. But considering the realities of life, inevitably there will be times when children tangle over some incident. Sometimes one child will hit another, or grab a toy. Then there is the need for conflict resolution.

A few years ago we were given some good advice by a school counselor. He said, "When a child hits, do not ask why. The child will inevitably give a reason, and in his own mind he has justified his own action. The better approach," said the counselor, "is to state simply, 'We cannot have hitting because it hurts.' " Then if the children are able to talk about their disagreement, it is good to let them speak directly to each other. The more that the children resolve their own conflicts, the more permanently they grow in ways of coping. But if one or both are too upset to talk, then there needs to be a "cooling off" period. The offender needs to sit alone to

think about the seriousness of his or her deed. If there has been damage, the offender needs to repair it. The more the consequence is logical, the more meaning is made from the incident.

But if there is nothing to repair, the offender could sit a few minutes to think about his or her actions. We use a small egg timer, an hour glass with sand, so the offender can sit and wait till all the sand goes through before resuming play. Or if the child cannot play constructively that day, we may say, "Today it appears that you are not ready for the block corner; perhaps you need to read in the book corner. Tomorrow perhaps you will be ready to play again in the block corner." As long as we use the term "ready," we are not saying that anybody is "bad." We are implying that though some growing is needed, there is no doubt but that this individual child will reach the goal of happy social interaction at a later time.

Often parents tell us of sending a child to his or her room for some offence. While the idea of a "cooling off" period is valid, as we have stated, the wisdom of using the bedroom as the "cooling off" place is questionable. To do so is to give many unhappy associations with the bedroom, so that it is no longer pleasant to go there to go to sleep at night. It is much better to have a "thinking chair" in the main portion of the home, so that the offending child can watch an egg timer run its sand through or sit in silence in the mainstream of the home. Then the bedroom remains a place for pleasant dreams.

When a child has been hit, or offended in some way, it is important for that child to use words to tell the offender how he or she feels. This kind of honest communication is not a screaming tirade aimed at the other person, but a direct telling of how one feels. A child might say "I have really angry feelings because you pushed me down and it hurt." The use of words to express feelings is a tremendously important art that can be practiced for the rest of a lifetime.

"Trust, Autonomy, and Initiative"

The author Erik Erikson has delineated eight tasks in life that the emotionally healthy person must accomplish. Three of these tasks pertain to the preschool years: developing trust, experiencing autonomy, and asserting initiative. The first of these emotional tasks is to develop a sense of trust. Trust grows during infancy years as a child is consistently loved, fondled, and fed. When an infant senses that he or she can depend on persons to feed, bathe, and clothe him or her, that child is well directed toward the development of this basic sense of trust.

Trust grows not only from the consistency of care, but also from the *attitude* of the caretaker. Babies, like puppy dogs, sense the way you feel about them. They know if care is motivated by love, or if it is just a chore. The unspoken relatedness, the sense of purposefulness, on the part of parents is communicated at deep levels to infants, and trust grows from a feeling of wholesome and joyous relatedness. Of course there are days when the work becomes a chore. There are days when the parents or caretakers are tired and would rather be asleep than up changing a diaper. But the general tone of caring, of interest in and love for the infant, is the main message that is communicated in the early years of a child's life, and it is those basic attitudes of parental love and dependability that enable a baby to develop a sense of trust.

By the time a child comes to preschool, the basic development of trust should already be well under way. But if a child arrives who is unduly fearful, then teachers and other caretakers have the challenge of trying to edge that child along the continuum from mistrust to trust. Extra love and care will need to be showered upon that child. And even for basically trustful children there is still the need to consolidate and extend the sense of trust.

An atmosphere that builds for trust is one in which promises are kept. If a teacher or parent says, "Tomorrow we will . . . ," then it is absolutely vital that tomorrow we do just as we promised. The atmosphere that builds for trust is as necessary in a home, day care center, or nursery school as is food for growing bodies.

Suppose we say to the children, "Tomorrow we will see again the pictures in this filmstrip." Suppose that the next day we get hurried and forget that we have made this commitment. We might even reason to ourselves that the children have already seen this filmstrip once so it is not too important to show it again. But the important consideration is that we have said that we would show it, and the children are remembering our words. If for some unexpected reason we cannot show the filmstrip—perhaps the projector is broken—then we can explain our reason and plan to show the filmstrip another day. Whatever we do, we must not leave a promise dangling! An explained change of plans is understandable only in a climate where a strong sense of trust has already been established. Building attitudes of trust is the most basic task for emotional growth. Faith grows from trust, and trust is the prerequisite!

Routines can be a source of trust building. Children need a consistency of programming so that they can know what to expect. At nursery school, for instance, the day progresses generally from the creative play hour to group time, then snack time, then rest time, then outdoor time. The child feels the rhythm of the day and internalizes a sense of order and develops a trustful feeling. When there is necessity for a departure from routine, it is carefully explained so that the child can anticipate and understand.

Once the three-year-olds from Eden Laboratory School took a morning trip to the zoo. They returned to nursery school just in time for the

mothers to take the children home. One little girl, (who had never before been very interested in rest time) said, "We can't go home yet, we haven't taken out our mats for rest time." Her internal sense of order in the daily activities was calling for routine even in the midst of special excitement.

Beyond the sense of trust is the need for autonomy. Autonomy is the chance to do something independently. Toddlers want to "do their own thing" in order to experiment with life and learn what it is all about. Among the first words a child says will be the phrase "me do," or "all by myself."

It isn't easy to grant all the reckless requests of a toddler. The messes we have to clean after the soup is spilled and the pudding is all over the face may discourage our allowance of autonomy for the small child. But within safe and reasonable limits, the child of ages 1-3 must have a chance to do many things independently, including self-feeding, and exploration of a large area of space. When we limit a toddler too closely, we stifle that child's inborn motivation to learn what the world is all about.

Small children actually have a need to be messy. If we keep them too prim and clean we may be doing untold damage. Naturally, we cannot let them live in unhygienic surroundings, but we can plan socially acceptable ways for the child to be messy. We can plan for finger painting, for water play, for smearing a tabletop with shaving cream, for "gooey gluey" activities, and for as many other unstructured events as our creative-minds can foster. When a child invents a messy activity, our first question is "is it safe?" and if the answer is to the affirmative our next response can be "why not?" There are limits, of course, to "messy activities" but within the reasonable limits these chances to daub and pat and smear a variety of substances are vital chances for the task of autonomy.

More sophisticated than autonomy is the assertion of initiative. This task comes into play during the ages of 3-6, and it involves creative play and work within a framework of responsibility. Autonomy was the reckless onslaught of a toddler, but initiative is the more refined expression of growing abilities in preschoolers. The rigid independence of age two, with its preponderance of language centering around "me" should give way at age three to the more "eager to please" activities, when language has a more "I will" flavor. Initiative is seen in the building of elaborate block structures, in the making of esthetically pleasing paintings or collage designs, and in fanciful role play simulating adult life.

Initiative is expressed in a variety of creative activities. One of the most basic of these for preschoolers is the making of collages. A collage is an assortment of bits and pieces glued to a background. There can be an endless variety of collage items, ranging from bits of cloth cut from a scrap bag, to bits of junk saved from a workbench. Bits of paper, bits of packing material, items from the world of nature—all are good for collage making.

Initiative can be asserted in language development, as a child "writes" a story or poem. Or a group of children can "write up" a report of a trip to the bakery. Children need the chance to assert themselves responsibly in an atmosphere where their efforts can be noticed and appreciated. Once at Eden Laboratory School a group of children decided to have a "trumpet band" after they had been visited by a man with a trumpet.

Taking the long hollow rods from the "Giant Tinker Toy" set, they began blowing on the rods and making trumpet-like sounds. The teacher, Mrs. Ann Schroer, noticed this group initiative, and immediately played a rhythm record so that the children could have their band performance raised to a loud and successful conclusion!

We see, then, the progression of tasks from the building of trust, on through the experiencing of autonomy, and then to the assertion of initiative. By working at these preschool tasks, children grow in emotional health and wholeness.

Multi-ethnic Experiences

Since preschool years are the span of life when most attitudes are formed, they are ripe times for children to get to know and appreciate persons from a variety of cultures. It is fortunate if a nursery school or day care center can have children enrolled from a variety of ethnic groups. Then there can be a natural sharing of experiences—children can learn of special foods, songs, stories, games, and dress of other cultures. The parents of the children in a multi-ethnic setting can be valuable resource persons as they visit and play with the children.

The curriculum can be greatly enriched if other persons from diverse cultures can be invited in. Perhaps the children can have a unit on Japanese culture, in which they make decorations of paper lanterns, cook sukiyaki in the classroom, listen to Japanese music, and do some simple paper folding *(origami)*. Then the highlight of the unit will be the day when a Japanese visitor comes, wearing a brightly-colored kimono, and telling about her experiences as a child in Japan.

Or there can be a unit on Mexico, with the making of tacos, the making of paper serapes, the dancing of the "Hat Dance," and culminating in a visit by a person from Mexico. African units, also, are deeply meaningful as the children print their own "dashikis" from pieces of old sheets, sing songs with African rhythms, and cook "peanut soup." For an African unit, once, we had the good fortune of having a visitor from Ethiopia. The visitor told folk tales of his native land to the children who sat on the rug at his feet absolutely spellbound by his presentation.

In the homes, it is of utmost value to have dinner guests from other countries. A parent told recently of how she called a local university to see if there were any foreign students who could come to her home for dinner. To her delight, a young couple from India accepted her invitation. Her children are still talking about the lady who came to dinner, in her beautiful long sari. Such an event is enriching for the family and for the couple who comes to dinner. It is out of this kind of friendly intercultural communication that attitudes of mutual appreciation grow, and world peace has seeds of hope planted.

Making and Cultivating Friendships

Basic to all social-emotional development is the making and cultivation of friendships. Children need peer play to grow and develop. Studies from the University of Wisconsin, where rhesus monkeys are raised in isolation, show that these primates will not mate in adult years if they have not had previous opportunities to play with their age mates. Children need one another in the healthy growing process.

Children also need to associate with persons of other age ranges. Older children feel delight with the chance to help bathe a baby. They also feel delight at the chance to visit grandmother or to talk to some older person. Actually, the relatedness between a small child and a senior citizen is one of life's most rewarding experiences. There is something special about the association between children and grandparents. Where grandparents are not available, other persons of that age should be brought into the child's home or classroom.

Perhaps there is a retired person who can come one day a week to the nursery school or day care center. This regular visit would be very meaningful for the children, and would also give the senior citizen a renewed awareness of his or her own value. It is deadly to think of how many older persons live in isolation in retirement centers or nursing homes, when children could be a part of their lives. One October a group of children from Eden Laboratory School went to parade in Halloweeen costumes at a local nursing home. The experience was beautiful because before the afternoon was over the children were sitting in the laps of their new-found friends. This kind of relatedness is mutually beneficial.

An article in a recent newspaper tells of how one nursery school adopted a policy of "grandparent power." The school actively solicited participation in the program from all interested grandparents. Another good possibility is for a nursery school to "adopt" a nearby nursing home and make regular visits, or send greeting cards (child-made, of course) on all special occasions. In this way, children develop friendships among persons of all ages.

Out of these friendships there should grow a sense of empathy—the

ability to share the feelings of others. When a child can be glad for another's joy, or be sad for another's disappointment, then real empathy is growing. It helps to talk about each other's feelings so that empathy can grow. The ability to share, also, grows from mutual friendships. The joy of sharing can come from sharing a toy, from learning to "take turns" on a tricycle, or the sharing of one's energies in making a "surprise" for the friends in the nursing home.

Moral Development

Dr. Lawrence Kohlberg from Harvard University has delineated for us the way persons grow in moral development. He tells us that an infant and a toddler are a-moral in the sense that they have no understanding of what is right and what is wrong. Being "a-moral" is not the same as being "immoral" for the latter is the condition of an older person who knows better but chooses to do what is wrong or hurtful. Infantile a-moral status is understandable.

As the child emerges from the reckless phases of toddler autonomy, the child learns the first lesson in moral behavior: namely to "do good" to avoid punishment. Now this first step in moral development does not involve an inner awareness of the reason for "right" and "wrong" acts, but merely reflects adult standards and the need to conform to avoid punishment.

A little higher on the ladder of moral growth is the desire to "do good" to get a reward. Early in life a child learns that if he or she does something pleasing, there will be a smile or a kind word from an adult observer. So children learn to conform to get the satisfaction of approval. If a one-year-old were left alone in a room with a birthday cake, that child might just grab a fist-full of cake with no understanding of the need to wait for the party to begin. This is a-moral behavior.

On the child's second birthday there might be the advanced behavior of leaving the cake alone because to demolish it would bring punishment. At age three the child would wait patiently (or impatiently but would wait) because by leaving the cake alone there was the assurance of the reward of a happy birthday party with ice cream and presents.

This birthday cake analogy is a way of showing the progression of moral development. Preschool years are when a child learns what is expected of him or her, and generally conforms out of fear of punishment or hope of reward. But such primitive morality is all external. It involves little understanding of *why* certain actions are considered proper and others are not acceptable. Unless a child goes on to internalize his own standards of behavior, that child will never grow to moral maturity. Thus we see the need for the growth of conscience in the child, and at age five this process should have some impetus.

How can we help a child reason at higher levels? How can we help a child understand that other people have rights, too, and that it is just as important for them to get what they need as for our own wishes to be granted? Dr. Kohlberg believes that children develop conscience from "wrestling with moral dilemmas." He believes that children need the chance to decide what would be right in a number of situations. Adults who talk with children can help them figure out what would be "fair" and what would be "unfair" in various situations. But the sense of moral justice grows from the child's own reasoning about what to do in a certain situation. It will not grow if the child is always told what to do with no chance to explore alternatives.

Open-ended stories for discussion are the best tools for moral development according to Dr. Kohlberg. A story can be told, for instance, about a child who broke a friend's tricycle accidentally. To avoid punishment, the child ran home, and nobody knew she had broken it. But then the child thought about how the friend might try to ride the tricycle, not knowing it was broken, and get hurt. What should the child do? If she told that she broke it, she might get punished. If she did not tell, her friend might get hurt. What should she do? Letting the children decide is the kind of opportunity they need in order to "exercise moral muscles" and grow to higher stages of moral reasoning.

Further up the ladder of moral reasoning (in children of about elementary school age) there will be the ability to act out of a sense of justice and fair play. In fact there will be a meticulously legalistic stage when children feel everything has to be exactly fair. A piece of cake divided has to be "absolutely equal" so that both persons get a fair share. This kind of rigid legalism of elementary years should give way in teen years to a new awareness that fairness is based on need as well as equality. Sometimes people *need* more than others, and therefore higher reasoning will consider needs as well as equal exchange.

The point is that children grow in moral decision making only as they have a chance to come to grips with what to do in a number of situations. Stories for children to finish often can offer such chances. Guidance Associates has filmstrips that give such open-ended stories. They come in a packet titled *First things: the strategy* (See bibliography for other resources along this line.) But stories you make up yourself for the children to finish can be the very best tools in moral development.

Summary

Social-emotional development is a long and complicated process, and in this chapter we have seen it evolving through a number of components. We have stressed the need for gender identification and sex-role freedom, the development of self-esteem, the opportunity to talk about feelings, good conflict resolution, "trust, autonomy and initiative," multi-ethnic experiences, making and cultivating friendships, and moral development. It is both challenging and rewarding to interact with young children and to see them moving toward more and more mature levels of social interaction.

Chapter Three

Nurturing Spiritual Growth

We were sitting on a rug listening to the custodian play Christmas carols on his trumpet. There was a captivating atmosphere of awe among the children and adults who were listening in rapt attention. Scott, barely four years old, who happened to be sitting next to me, took my hand and kissed the top of it. I looked down to smile at him and suddenly sensed that his action was a symbol of something wondrous that was happening in the whole room. There was an unspoken sense of elation, an expression of the inexpressible, a heightened awareness of Divine Presence.

This incident is an indication of what Dr. James Fowler meant when he stated that small children have "an intuitive appreciation of the qualitative distinctness of the numinous."*(1974, p. 214).* Look into a small child's face as he gazes at a rose, a caterpillar, or a thistle. The wonder and delight give off a glow that comes from the child's inner realization that something or Someone marvelous is at work. This glow is really an aura—an emanation of wonder and marvel, and an intuitive rapport with the deepest realities of life. There is an element of ecstacy—of joy, of enthusiasm at work in the small child's relatedness to the wondrous. A sense of splendor shining through the world is the gift the small child brings.

The poet, William Wordsworth was convinced of this fact, and he wrote these lines in "Ode: Intimations of Immortality from Recollections of Early Childhood":

"There was a time when meadow, grove and stream,
The earth, and every common sight,
To me did seem
Apparelled in celestial light,
The glory and the freshness of a dream . . . .

Our birth is but a sleep and a forgetting:
The soul that rises with us, our life's star,
Hath had elsewhere its setting,
And cometh from afar:
Not in entire forgetfulness,
And not in utter nakedness,
But trailing clouds of glory do we come
From God who is our home:
Heaven lies about us in our infancy!"

The sense of splendor, which in Judaism is called the "Shekinah" or the "glory of God" is a special quality in the small child's life which we wish to nurture. What will happen is that we will feel our own ultimate relatedness grow as we enhance it in the small child.

In this chapter, we approach this task through three emphases: Nurturing the sense of wonder, teaching through touching and trusting, and symbolizing in celebrations.

Nurturing the Sense of Wonder

What do we mean by the term "wonder"? Dr. Sam Keen in his book *Apology for Wonder* defines it as:

> "The capacity for sustained and continued delight, marvel, amazement, and enjoyment. It is the capacity of the child to approach the world as if it were a smorgasbord of potential delights, waiting to be tasted. It is the sense of freshness, anticipation, and openness that rules the life of a healthy child." *(Keen, 1969, p. 43.)*

Then he goes on to say that a specific type of wonder is the objective of spiritual nurture. This special type is the wonder *that* there could be such amazing sights and events in the world. To wonder *that* is not the same as to wonder *why.* it is profitable for scientific purposes to wonder *why* certain phenomena occur, but it is more profitable for spiritual purposes to wonder *that* they occur. The goal of spiritual nurture, then, is to increase the child's ability to wonder *that* there should be such creatures as bees, mules, and giraffes!

Dr. Keen says:

> "Wonder and awe are closely associated with the experience of the holy. . . . I will suggest further that there is no substantial difference between wonder and the experience of the holy." *(Ibid. p. 35.)*

Adults can learn a lesson from children, as they venture together into the world of nature. But children also benefit from adults who sustain and uphold this delight and reverence for life.

Rachel Carson, in her book *The Sense of Wonder,* makes the plea for adults to nurture the child's ability to wonder. She states:

> "If a child is to keep alive his inborn sense of wonder . . . he needs the companionship of at least one adult who can share it, rediscovering with him the joy, excitement, and mystery of the world we live in." *(Carson, 1956, p. 45.)*

Having read from these authors, we plan for the children in our school to experience as many wonders as possible. Sometimes we take the children out on field trips such as to Grant's farm, or to a pumpkin patch to experience wonders. At other times, we endeavor to bring wonders into the classroom. Wonders thus can be seen in beans growing in a jar, or radishes growing in a planting box.

Wonders are beheld in animal friends who visit the school (once the Humane Society brought some magnificent rabbits for a visit), or in gerbils who live in cages in the classroom and frequently have baby gerbils!

Blowing milkweed pods into the air, blowing soap bubbles, dancing with balloons and scarves, or "foot painting" on a long sheet of wrapping paper all give the sense of exhilaration that is an experience of wonder. Once a teacher brought in some blank film leader and let the children mark on it with felt markers. At rest time she ran it through an eight millimeter projector, and played music to accompany the lines that danced and undulated across the screen from the children's markings. There was a sense of awe that day—a delight unspeakable that something so creative had happened, right there in their own classroom.

Brother Gabriel Moran, F.S.C., in his book *Design for Religion* states: "If Christian faith has a future it will issue from a way of looking at the world that stimulates response, creativity, and passionate involvement," *(p. 87).* Indeed, we teach a spiritual lesson when we have a wondrous experience that is spirited and shared with enthusiasm. The very word "enthusiasm" comes from the root words "en" and "theos" meaning "in God." The response in enthusiasm is the response that is spirited.

The response in "perpetual surprise" is just the opposite of boredom or taking life for granted. Rabbi Abraham Joshua Heschel in his book *Between God and Man,* states that, "Wonder and radical amazement is the chief characteristic of the religious man's attitude toward history and nature." *(1959, p. 41).*

It is true that adults perceive wonder a bit differently than children do.

As Dr. Keen points out, adults wonder at vast landscapes while children wonder at small details. This fact is not at all surprising in view of the fact that (as explained in Chapter One) the child has not yet "decentered" his attention from the small detail. Also, the child stands closer to the ground, and sees the immediate more than the distant scene. It is not at all unusual for a child to be concentrating on an earthworm while his mother is looking over the whole garden! Perhaps the child's eyes are even keener than the older person's eyes, and younger eyes detect intricate details better. Regardless of the explanation, it is good to notice how the focus of wonder differs between children and adults. But it is even more important to realize that the *process* of wonder is the same: to behold, to delight, to cherish, indeed to be caught up on a spirit of ecstacy! Children and adults need one another in the realization of this spiritual experience.

The inner realization of wonder needs outer expression occasionally. The need is not for "preachy" wordiness, and not for over-extended talks, but quiet tribute in a few sentences such as, "Isn't it a wonder that God has made such a creature as a hummingbird!" These brief exclamations, like punctuation marks in a sentence, heighten the experience, increase the awareness, and bring the happening into focus. Spontaneous prayers—especially "thank you" prayers—culminate the religious experience.

Sometimes appropriately selected books will help in the verbalization of wonder. A few favorites along this line, which we use at Eden Laboratory School are: *Isn't it a Wonder?* by Carrie Lou Goddard, and *Wonderful Child* by Jill Jackson. This second book has a record with it and the music is as enchanting as the words and photography. Another favorite is *God and Me* by Florence Heide. Other books of this type are listed in the bibliography, but the parent or teacher will do well to keep abreast of the new publications, choosing with careful selectivity the ones which stress the wonder and delight of the world around us, and the warmth of human encounter.

Teaching through Touching and Trust

Spiritual development is not completed in the wondrous beholding of nature, it is only begun. Next there is the development of faith through personal relatedness with other people. Small children think, act, and feel all at the same time. Their relatedness to God is both nurtured and expressed in their relatedness to persons. A child "acts out" his faith in his affection to persons—in a hug, a kiss, and in quiet time just sitting in a large person's lap. We cherish each time that the child can touch or be touched by persons who care. Indeed, it seems impossible for faith to grow in an atmosphere devoid of human relatedness.

In the home and in the nursery, one of the most important tools for religious education is the rocking chair! Dr. Martin Buber, in his book *I and Thou,* makes the statement, "Every particular Thou is a glimpse through to the Eternal Thou." *(1937, p. 75).* He is saying that persons are windows through whom God can be seen and realized. The religious relatedness, then, becomes like a triangle in which a person perceives God through another person. Faith, then, can be diagrammed as a triangle, or as Dr. James Fowler states:

> "Perhaps it is more accurate to say faith is *tri-polar.* For it is a sense of relatedness to the ultimate condition of existence which simultaneously informs and qualifies our relations and interactions with the mundane, the everyday, the world of persons and things." *(1973, p. 208).*

Once a child has learned to love and trust humans, he is well on his way toward developing love and faith in God.

Love is expressed in times of joy, when it is buoyant and uplifting. But it needs to be expressed also at times of crises. When a child has been hurt or disappointed, he needs the reassurance that somebody understands and is concerned. Something of the divine pathos, like God watching over the Children of Israel in Egypt, needs to be exemplified in the adults who affect the lives of children today. Children must know that adults care and are concerned.

The child who has been offended needs to be swooped up into loving arms. The child who has done the offending also needs love, although that child also needs to know clearly which behaviors are unacceptable. Grace may be intuitively felt, even when it is not rationally understood. Justice may demand that the offender sit alone, away from the group, until she or he has learned to cope with the situation. Or the offender may need to mend what has been broken or otherwise right the wrong.

Once Amy marred the walls of the nursery school by scribbling on them with crayon, even though she knew that her action would not be acceptable. We talked with Amy about how much we enjoy clean walls, and suggested that she help scrub off all the crayon marks. With sponge, water, and cleanser, Amy worked at the wall for the rest of the "free play" period. We helped, occasionally, where it took strength to remove a particular mark, but by and large Amy did most of the work. It was not a punishment, *per se,* it was "logical consequences" that when we dirty the wall we need to clean it. At one point in the procedure, Amy said "I'm missing all the fun," to which we replied casually, "yes, it is more fun to play than to scrub." But at the end of the period the wall was finished, bright and clean as ever, and Amy sighed a deep sigh of relief and hugged us, saying, "We did it, didn't we—we fixed it all right again!"

This little incident had deep religious overtones, because it involved both justice and love, and the deep realization that while an offence is unacceptable, the offender is still a beloved child of God.

A prerequisite of faith is trust. If the home, daycare center, or nursery school is a place where promises are kept, the way is open for trust and faith to grow. But if as parents and teachers we become careless in our promises—perhaps figuring the child will not remember, we may be doing untold damage to faith development.

So far we have discussed spiritual nurture through the sense of wonder, and through relatedness to persons. But there are many beliefs in the Judeo-Christian heritage that are essential to the whole western tradition and the need to be learned in other ways. We turn now to ways of learning faith through celebrations that symbolize and dramatize deep underlying meanings in life.

Symbolizing in Celebrations

As faith is growing, it becomes reinforced in the symbolic actions of the home and the community. There are two basic types of celebration that nurture growing faith: the "rights of passage" celebrating special times in each individual's life pilgrimage, and the calendar celebrations that occur at intervals during the year to observe times of special meaning in the community.

Examples of the rites of passage are: Baptism, Confirmation, First Communion, Marriage, Holy Orders or ordination, and Anointing of the Sick or last rites. In the Jewish tradition, the Bar Mitzvah for boys and Bas Mitzvah for girls are rites of passage marking the end of childhood and the beginning of responsible participation in the life of the community. Actually, each birthday celebration also is a part of the rites of passage.

It is very important that each child's birthday be celebrated. Birthday parties become ways of recognizing that the child is important, and that he or she is growing larger and more responsible. The self esteem of a child grows as friends and adults gather to honor that child's birthday. At Eden Laboratory School we celebrate each child's birthday with a song, special "treats," and usually a "crown" for the honored child. If a child's birthday falls at a time when school is not in session, we pick a day to celebrate his or her "un-birthday!" In this way, each child has one special day in the school year.

Many events from the Judeo-Christian heritage are celebrated during the school year at Eden Laboratory School. These calendar events begin early in October with the Festival of Booths called Succot, a special Jewish expression of Thanksgiving. Actually, the instructions for this celebration are in the Book of Leviticus of the Bible, so all in the whole Judeo-Christian heritage are instructed to participate.. Leviticus 23:39-43 describes the feast of booths, and Deuteronomy 16:13-15 gives further reference. Nehemiah 8:13-18 tells of the people Israel remembering to celebrate this ancient tradition.

To re-enact this Festival of Booths, one needs a booth which can be decorated. The booth can be constructed from branches or lumber, and decorated with fruits of the harvest. At Eden Laboratory School there is a wooden climber that is the right size for a booth, so it is decorated to be the booth for the occasion. Decorations are made from colored construction paper—circles of orange to represent oranges, circles of red to represent apples, clusters of small purple circles to represent grapes, crescent-shaped yellow to represent bananas. The children cut these shapes from the paper and affix them on the booth with scotch tape. Across the top of the booth, the children place willow branches.

Meanwhile at group time the children are told the story which this event celebrates. To keep the story understandable to preschoolers, we use words such as these:

> A long, long time ago the people of Israel were travelling from Egypt, where they had been slaves, toward Canaan, where they would be free. On their long journey, they had to camp out in the wilderness, and at first they feared that they would have no food to eat. There were no stores at all where they were camping. Their leader, Moses, prayed that he would know what to do to help his people find food.
>
> When evening came, many quails came and flew into the area where the people of Israel could catch them, and roast them for dinner. And the next morning, there was a dew on the ground and small bits of food like bread were on the ground so that the people could gather and eat them. They called this special kind of bread "manna." Thus the people of Israel had enough food to eat, even in the wilderness, and they thanked God for the food.
>
> Now it is 3000 years later, but to remember that wonderful way that food was found in the wilderness, the people still build booths, the size of camping tents, and eat their meals in them for seven days. The Jewish people, who are the people of Israel, decorate their booths with fruits and branches this time of year and get inside the booths to feast and say "thank you" to God. Often they read psalms of praise in their booths as a way of giving thanks for the food that was given to Moses and the people of Israel long ago and also to say "thank you" for the harvest of fruits today at this time of the year.

When the booth is decorated and the children understand the story, a teacher and a few children at a time go into the booth. They eat fruit, as the teacher reads Psalm 9, verses 1 and 2: "I will give thanks to the Lord with my whole heart; I will tell of thy wonderful deeds. I will be glad and exult in thee. I will sing praise to thy name, O Most High." Any other verse, that is a psalm of praise, can be used. Just casual conversation on how good the fruit tastes can be a very meaningful part of the celebration.

The next calendar event that is celebrated is Halloween. For this event, pumpkins are made into jack-o-lanterns and special orange and black decorations are hung around the room. Children are asked to wear costumes, with *no masks* on the day of Halloween. Then there is a parade through the building, as the children knock on doors to play "trick or treat" on all who work in the school building (which is also a church). The children sing songs for the persons in the offices, and receive "treats." Then there may be a halloween *pinata,* stuffed with treats, which the children use in celebration. The *pinata* is hung from the ceiling or on the outdoor climber, and one by one the children hit it with a stick until it breaks and the contents "rain" down for children to gather.

In November there is the celebration of Pilgrim Thanksgiving. Before we begin preparation for our reenactment of the historic event, we tell the story behind the celebration. In general, the wording of the story is simplified this way:

> Many years ago—more than

350 years ago—the Pilgrim people came across the ocean to this land to live. They came in a ship called the Mayflower. The first winter in this land those people had very little to eat. Some people say they had only five grains of corn a piece each day to eat. Times were very hard for these people.

But the friendly Indians who lived on this land showed the Pilgrim people how to grow corn and other vegetables, and how to catch wild turkeys and other meat out of the woods. So by the fall of the next year there was so much food that the Pilgrim people decided to have a special feast. They invited their Indian friends, to thank them for helping them have this food. Together, the Pilgrims and the Indians sat down to eat the feast and to thank God for such plenty. Every year since that time, people in this land have a special feast in the fall of the year and thank God for giving us enough to eat. This feast is called Thanksgiving.

After telling the story, we let the children play-act the landing of the Mayflower on the shores of this land. They build ship decks out of the large hollow blocks in the block corner, and they pretend they are Pilgrims first coming to these shores.

Costumes for the occasion are made from construction paper—tall black hats with silver buckles for the men and white bonnets and wide white collars for the women. The children help put costumes together. Then begins the preparation of the food. Some classrooms bake pumpkin pies, some make cranberry bread. Other children help cut up raw vegetables. The popcorn popper is busy getting more food ready for the feast. Then on the day before the Thanksgiving vacation, some children dress as Indians and some dress as Pilgrims by putting on the paper costumes. Meanwhile a row of tables has been covered with white paper and the feast is spread. The children sit at the tables, a prayer of thanksgiving is said or sung, and the feast begins. The value of this experience is that the children are interiorizing the feeling of the event, catching the spirit of celebration in Pilgrim Thanksgiving tradition.

The month of December offers the occasion to celebrate Hanukkah, the Jewish Festival of Lights. Before we begin our celebration, we tell the story:

> Long, long ago, the people of Israel had been conquered by a cruel king, who would not let them worship God in their Temple. They were very sad and worried. But there were among the people of Israel some very brave and clever persons who found a way to drive the cruel king out of their land. Then they were free to worship God again in their Temple.
>
> But when they went to the Temple, they found that there was only enough oil in the light to last one day, and it takes eight days to get the right kind of new oil ready. Sadly they lit the little bit of oil in the 'ner tamid' which is the special Temple light. They expected it to burn out and leave the Temple in darkness at the end of the day. But do you know what?
>
> That little bit of oil kept on glowing in the 'ner tamid' the next day and the next and the next—all eight days until the new oil was ready. The people of Israel, who are also called the Jewish people, said to one another 'This must be God's way of saying to us that He will always be with us.' They were very happy, and decided to plan ways that they could always remember the oil that burned eight days, and how much this happening meant to them.
>
> That event happened over 2100 years ago but today, still, the Jewish people celebrate to remember it. The way they celebrate is to have a special candle holder, called a *menorah,* with eight candles in a row as a reminder of the eight days the oil burned in the Temple. On the menorah there is another candle, taller than the rest, that is used to light the other candles. Just this time of the year, when this Festival of Lights called Hanukkah is celebrated, the Jewish families place their *menorahs* in their windows. On the first night of Hanukkah, they light one candle. On the second night of Hanukkah, they light two candles. On the third night of Hanukkah—can you guess?—they light three candles. And so on till all eight candles are burning brightly on the eighth night of Hanukkah. The families give presents to each member each night of Hanukkah. And as the candles are glowing in the Jewish homes, the children play a game with a little top called a *dreydel.* They spin the top, and the Hebrew letters on the top are the initials of a sentence that reminds everyone that "A great miracle happened there."

Immediately following the story, the teachers show the children a Jewish Hanukkah menorah, and help them light the "shamos" or "lighter candle" and then from it, one child lights the first candle of Hanukkah. The traditional Jewish prayer of thanks is said: "Blessed are you, Lord our God, King of the Universe, who sanctified us with your commandments and commanded us to kindle the lights of Hanukkah."

Than as candles glow in the menorah, the children are allowed to spin the dreydels, and also help the teachers prepare special food for the occasion. The special food for Hanukkah is potato pancakes, called latkes. These can be made from a commercial mix, or prepared as follows:

Grate and drain three cups of raw potatoes.
Grate four tablespoons of raw onion.
Beat two eggs.
Mix potatoes, onion, eggs, and one teaspoon salt, 1/2 teaspoon pepper and two tablespoons of cracker or matzo meal.
Drop mixture by tablespoons into a skillet 325 degrees with 1/2 cup oil, and brown on both sides.
Serve with applesauce or sour cream, (or sprinkle with cinnamon and eat).

When the latkes are ready, the children eat them, as the candles glow and perhaps some Hanukkah music is playing on the record player. Then for the next seven days, an additional candle is lit each day in the menorah.

The days preceding Christmas are devoted to capturing a feeling for the real meaning of the season. The whole emphasis is upon Christmas as a celebration of Jesus' birthday, and the wonder and tenderness of the manger scene. The story is read from the second chapter of the book of Luke, and from carefully selected picture books. Then it is retold, simply, in words such as these:

Many, many years ago in a land far away, Mary and Joseph were travelling to the little town of Bethlehem to arrange to pay their taxes. It was a long journey, and since there were no automobiles in those days the only way they could travel was to walk or to ride their donkey. Their feet were very tired from travelling so far over the dusty roads. Mary was especially tired, because she was about to have a baby.

As they got near to the town of Bethlehem, they stopped to see the town in the distance. Joseph said: "Surely there will be an inn—a hotel—in Bethlehem, where we can sleep during the night."

Mary said: "And surely the inn will have a stable where our donkey can spend the night."

But when they came to the door of the inn in Bethlehem, the innkeeper said: "No. I do not have any room for you in the inn. All my rooms are already filled with people."

Joseph explained that they were very tired, and that Mary was soon to have a baby. The innkeeper then said: "Well, if you have to have a place to lie down, you can go out into the stable, where cows and donkeys sleep, and you can sleep on the hay."

Mary and Joseph and their donkey went out to the stable, and they lay down on the pile of hay. There were animals all around them, but all were sleeping. Then during the night a most wonderful thing happened: Mary gave birth to her baby, and they wrapped him in cloths and laid him in a manger to sleep on the hay.

Meanwhile on a distant hill, shepherds who were watching their sheep felt a special radiance and gladness for the message which they received about the birth of the baby in Bethlehem. They said to one another, "Let's go over to Bethlehem to see this special baby who is sleeping in a manger." So the shepherds went quickly into the town of Bethlehem, and found Mary and Joseph, and the baby Jesus lying in a manger. With great excitement the shepherds gazed at the newborn child and told Mary and Joseph that they knew the baby would grow up to show God's love in a most special way.

The wonder of that night of nights was expressed in the bright light of a star that led wise men of the East to come to Bethlehem and bring gifts to the newborn baby. And even though that happened almost 2000 years ago, we remember the birth of Jesus every time that we celebrate Christmas. Though we are not able to see Jesus today, we celebrate his birthday by giving gifts to persons we love, remembering the words of the Shepherds: "Jesus came to show God's love in a most special way."

After the story is told, the children are invited to act it out, using simple costumes that have been hung on the dress-up rack. Children choose parts, one being Mary, one being Joseph, some being shepherds, and some being wise men. And of course there is a choice role for the "inn-keeper." A manger is made by placing real hay in a box, or in the wooden doll bed. An inn is constructed from large blocks from the block corner. Then simply, as a teacher reads again the story, the children walk through their parts, catching the feeling of the wonder of this special event.

The story is acted, and re-enacted many times, so that every child gets a chance to act every part that she or he desires. Once as we were choosing parts a small boy asked if he could play the part of Mary. We agreed that in a drama anybody can play any part, and Peter was delighted to put on the white robe of Mary, and later to place the Jesus doll tenderly in the manger. The wonder comes through in the feeling tone of the enactment, and in the realization that such a special baby should be born in such a lowly place as a stable for cattle.

It is not long before the children begin using their own words for the conversations in the story, so that the teacher merely stands by to help whenever needed. For several days before Christmas, the children "play act" the nativity story, storing up in their innermost selves the deep meaning of the season.

Other ways of observing the Christmas season are the baking of Christmas cookies, the making of presents for parents, and the decorating of a tree which the children have helped bring into the classroom. At the nursery school, we do not have a Santa Claus because our focus is on celebrating Jesus' birthday. If the children mention Santa, we reply that Santa is a jolly helper who helps us celebrate Jesus' birthday.

After the Christmas holidays, it is good to have a unit on the boyhood and the manhood of Jesus so that the children can understand that the special baby in the manger grew up to be the person who said, "Let the children come to me." One January when we had a seminary student working at the nursery school, we had an enactment of the account from Mark 10:13-16. A teacher pretended to be the mother of some children who were going to see Jesus. Another teacher played the part of a disciple who said, "Jesus is too busy to see the children." Then the seminary student, who had an appropriately bushy beard and mustache, took the role of Jesus and said, "Indeed, I am not too busy for children. Let the children come to me." Whereupon the children swarmed into his lap and he reached big brawny arms around them. It was truly a most tender scene, and it said nonverbally to the children that Jesus, who was born in a manger, grew up to be a person who showed love in a special way.

Although little is known of the boyhood of Jesus, much is known about the culture of Palestine in biblical times. Therefore it is possible to build a unit around the customs that abounded when Jesus grew up: the baking of bread in a brick oven, the life in houses with flat rooftops, and the work in a carpenter's shop. The unit can be multi-sensory as bread is baked and eaten with figs and dates and other dried fruits. This unit follows and rounds out the Christmas season. Some years we have also celebrated Epiphany with a pinata.

January 15 is the birthday of Dr. Martin Luther King, Jr. Each year a holiday is given in his honor, and the children are led into a realization of his importance. The following version

of his story is told to the children as they are gathered at group time: (A large picture of Dr. King is held up for the children to see as they listen)

Tomorrow we are going to have a holiday to celebrate the birthday of this great man. Let's look at his picture, and notice how kind his eyes look. He really cared about people. He was a minister at Dexter Avenue Baptist Church in Birmingham, Alabama a few years ago, and something happened that made him determined to do something helpful.

At that time there was a very unfair law. The law was written inside the door of each bus, and it said: "White patrons please seat from the front of the bus, colored patrons please seat from the rear." This unfair law meant that if a person had light skin he or she could sit at the front of the bus but if a person had dark skin he or she had to sit at the back of the bus. Now everybody paid the same amount of money to ride the bus, so it was very unfair that some people got the best seats and some people got worse seats or no place to sit at all. One day a lady named Rosa Parks paid her money and got on the bus. She was tired from a long day's work, and since there were no seats vacant in the back of the bus, she sat in the front of the bus even though her skin was dark. The bus driver said she could not do this.

Rosa Parks told her story to Dr. King who said, "We must do something to change the very unfair law. Lets gather everybody together and agree that we will not ride the buses any more until the law is changed." Dr. King then led the people in carrying out the plan. For more than a year—more than all the time you spend in nursery school—the people did not ride the buses. It was a hard time because many people had to walk to work, or share rides, or take taxis.

But finally the owners of the buses said, "We're not making any money. Maybe we had better change that law." So they made a new law that said anybody can ride on any seat of the bus. Then the people began riding the buses again. Dr. King had helped them get rid of the unfair law. This story is only one of many things that Dr. King did to help his people have a more fair way of life. And because he cared so much about people, we remember him by having a holiday to celebrate his birthday.

One year the children helped bake a cake to honor his birthday, even though they understood that he is not alive today. Pictures of this great man are kept in the classroom for several days in January.

In February, the birthdays of Abraham Lincoln and George Washington are celebrated, with pictures and stories from their lives. A log cabin is constructed from "Lincoln Logs" to help the children understand the way "Honest Abe" lived when he was growing up. The story of how he walked two miles to give back a penny that the store man had mistakenly given him is a favorite among the children at this time of year, as well as the story, of course, of George Washington and the cherry tree. Legendary though these stories may be, they symbolize the kind of character that these presidents exemplified in their lives.

Then comes Valentine's day, celebrated with bright red heart decorations and plenty of opportunity for each child to fashion special valentines for parents and friends. We like to have paper, scissors, and paste aplenty on the tables, and to let the children work individually rather than having to follow a pattern. If they need help in cutting a heart shape, help is given, of course. But it is the child's creativity that makes for the most meaningful valentine, and valentine box. Then valentines are exchanged when the Valentine party is held, along with special treats and much feeling of loving messages.

March brings St. Patrick's day, with bright green shamrocks around the room. Children love to paint the green on shamrock-shaped easel paper, or to make green shamrock-shaped prints on white construction paper. The story of the historic Patrick of Ireland can be told in the following version, even though as with all great people it is impossible to separate actual facts from legendary interpretations:

"Long ago Patrick lived near the seashore in Wales. When he was a young man, some persons from Ireland came and kidnapped Patrick and took him to their island to work as a herder of pigs. Patrick was not happy working as a slave for the people of Ireland, and he prayed that he could get free.

One day Patrick got the chance to escape from Ireland by taking a ship that was sailing to France. It was a ship carrying a cargo of dogs, and Patrick was allowed to ride the ship if he would take care of the dogs. In France, Patrick stayed in a monastery—a home for monks—which was a safe place to stay until he could arrange to go back to his own home in Wales.

It was good to be home again, and Patrick could have stayed there for the rest of his life. But he kept thinking of all he had learned in the monastery about God's love and about how God showed his love so specially in Jesus. Patrick decided that he must go and tell this message to the people in Ireland.

First Patrick went back to France to learn as much as he could about the Christian faith. Then he went to Ireland to spend the rest of his life telling people about God's love. Isn't that amazing that Patrick went to spend his life showing love to the very people who had once kidnapped him and who had made him work as a slave? Because of his special deeds, Patrick is honored today with the title of Saint. Ireland, where he lived, has lots of green shamrock plants growing on the land, and they look like clover. So when the day is set aside to honor Patrick, decorations abound in green colors." (Paraphrased from *Church of Our Fathers* by Roland Bainton)

Another custom appropriate for a St. Patrick's Day celebration is "the wearing of the green." Children have been asked to come wearing some items of green clothing as a way of remembering the green fields of Ireland.

When it is Easter season, it is time to celebrate "God's promise of new life." All the world is a parable of this promise at this season of the year, as old bulbs that have been buried in the ground all winter send up green shoots that burst into blossom. Baby chicks hatch from chicken eggs, and bare trees send forth tiny green buds. To the small child, the basic attitude of joy and praise at Easter time is of prime importance. In later years, knowledge and belief can grow on this firm foundation, but the attitude of wonder and joy at Easter is what is most needed in the life of a small child.

What, then, are appropriate ways of celebrating Easter with preschool children? Decorating the room with the brightly-painted egg-shaped papers is a good beginning. Dyeing hard-boiled eggs is fun and meaningful. Making Easter baskets from stiff paper, and decorating them is creative. If there are newborn animal babies nearby, it is good to take a trip to see them. The whole emphasis adds up to a joyful appreciation of the meaning of Easter as God's promise of new life.

At the nursery school we do not mention the "Easter Bunny." Somehow the Easter Bunny custom seems to mislead the children from the real emphasis of the season. And if we were to go along with endorsing the idea of a bunny who gives gifts, we might be damaging the later acceptance of the Easter event in its fullness.

Hiding and hunting eggs (providing the children know that it is a teacher who hides them) can be a zestful experience. Making Easter cards for parents is always meaningful. Songs of praise, well-selected for the ages of the children, can bring the season into focus.

An enactment prior to Easter that is especially meaningful is a Palm Sunday processional. The children are told that Jesus was greeted with the waving of scarves and palm branches when he came into Jerusalem. So children at the nursery school cut palm branches from green construction paper. Then at the appointed time, as one child "rides" a plywood donkey into the classroom the other children greet him with waving of scarves and palm leaves, and sounds of "hosanna."

After the Easter season, there is occasion for other springtime celebrations. Kite day is lilting, as the children make simple kites and go outdoors to fly them in the wind. There is a spirited exhilaration as children feel the wind lift their kites into the air.

May Day is a day that can usually be spent totally out of doors. Often at Eden Laboratory School we spend the first of May out in the play yard, dancing with balloons, flying paper bag kites, decorating the concrete with colored chalk and the fence with crepe paper streamers. Foot painting on long strips of butcher paper adds to the feeling of joy.

In this chapter, we have explored together many ways of celebrating those aspects of life that have the deepest meaning. We have by no means exhausted the subject. These suggestions are "for instance." Each home and each day care center or nursery school can weave together its own program of celebrations.

The important points to remember are that children appropriate a sense of values and a lasting faith from approaching life with wonder, from being close to adults who are trustworthy and loving, and from celebrating with enthusiasm and creativity those occasions which stand for the meaning messages of life.

Chapter 4

Promoting Physical Development

Danny enters the outdoor play area through the gate. He spends a brief moment surveying the scene, and then darts off to the area of the large conduit pipe. Several children are already inside, and Danny joins the procession of little bodies that wriggle through the pipe and run back to wriggle through again. When that game gets old, Danny climbs up on top of the pipe, slides off, and climbs up again. Some days he will sit on top of the pipe for a while, in a kind of pause between spurts of energy, and then he will be off again, this time to make his way to the top of the metal climber.

Informal Exercise

It is in this kind of informal exercise that the preschool child gets most of his muscle-stretching activity. Formal games and sports are usually more appropriate for older children. Undirected, but supervised, activity is the most appropriate physical development for the preschool child. The skill of the teacher or the parent shines forth in the way the play area is arranged. Does it look inviting to the child, so the interest level is high? Is there area for running, for jumping, for crawling under, for climbing over, and for digging? Do the items lead into imaginative play? Are all safety factors checked out so that no activity is hazardous? These kinds of questions have been considered by the adults in skillful planning of the play yard area.

Forethought can also be given to the quality of the imaginative play in the outdoor area. Hopefully the children will engage in adventurous games that do not include violence. In today's culture where television often conditions children toward gun play, it is our challenge as educators to encourage more constructive fantasy. What a windfall it was, at our nursery school, when a camp director donated an old row boat that was no longer seaworthy. On dry land in our play yard, that boat became a focus of creative play. Seated inside it, the children would ply imaginary oars back and forth calling out to one another,"Let's go to Noo-oo York!"

Commercial play equipment can be carefully selected for the children's use. It must be sturdy, challenging yet safe, and suitable for a variety of uses. The best equipment will not be too pictoral—rather, it will leave room for the child's imagination. A play house or a little log cabin can be the setting for much good dramatic play. One school placed the frame from an old "pick-up" truck on a play yard, after it had been carefully inspected for sharp edges or other harmful features. Children would climb into the driver's seat, while others would "load pumpkins" onto the back end.

When a school is on a limited budget, many discarded items can be used for the kind of informal exercise a child needs. Old tires to roll are full of fascination. Some children will even dare to get inside and "somersault" over as the tire rolls. Big boxes through which the children can crawl are among the best of equipment. Or the box can be made into a "house" when "windows" and "doors" are cut into it. The Learning Center in St. Louis, Missouri has classes for teachers in the art of "cardboard carpentry." Many items can be made from corrugated cardboard.

Tire climbers can be made by bolting tires on top of one another, pyramid fashion, and these climbers have the advantage of being not only inexpensive but also intriguing for the child's imagination. Large wooden spools which once held cable can be obtained for play use. Children can climb on them, or even learn to "walk" them as they turn. Barrels are fun, and can be put to good use for informal play—provided they have been carefully inspected to make sure that they are safe and splinter-free.

The parent and the teacher soon learn to salvage and improvise with many items for a fascinating play area. Railroad ties make dandy liners for a sand area or a planting area. Sections of telephone pole can be purchased inexpensively and used for the building of platforms or swing hangers. If a tree has been cut down, why not leave the stump for a jumping platform? Or leave a few of the log sections for the children to "walk."

In addition to climbing and swinging on permanent equipment, children also get enjoyment and benefit from riding on wheel toys such as tricycles and wagons. The purchase of such wheel toys can be made with a balance of activity in mind—so that there are vehicles to give leg exercise and other items to give the arm muscles a "work-out." Vehicles that can be used by several children together bring in a social value, as well as the physical use. For instance a wagon can involve the one who rides, the one who pushes, and the one who pulls. The wagon can then, in conversation, become a "steam engine," a "moving man," or a "tug boat" at the whisk of the imagination. Hardwood vehicles such as those manufactured by Community Playthings will last a long time and therefore merit the expense involved. Plastic vehicles such as "Big Wheel" are inexpensive, but may not survive more than one school year. There are advantages to having both types of equipment in a nursery school or daycare center.

A simple see-saw is good fun and

teaches reciprocity. Children learn as they ride, that when one end is up the other is down, and *vice versa.* "Jane's up, Sal's down," "Sal's up, Jane's down," the teacher calls out as two girls ride the see-saw. This activity is not only physical and social but also intellectual as the small child works at the preschool task of learning to think in reverse (See Chapter One).

For indoor play, blocks are among the most valuable of equipment. Hollow wooden blocks are standard for a four-year-old classroom. Though they involve an initial outlay of expense, they are long-lasting and precision-built. They stack evenly, and can be made into structures large enough for the children to get inside. Building and entering your own "house" gives a child a fresh perspective of himself or herself in relation to enclosed space. Stacking the blocks away at the end of a play period gives not only exercise but also a sense of order. When children work in cooperation on this kind of project, they learn cooperation as well as physical development.

Unit blocks are smaller hard wood blocks that are solid and come in a wide variety of shapes. There are triangles, rectangles, squares, cylinders, arches, and many other shapes in the unit block set. These blocks, too, are a very wise investment of initial expense because they are very durable and longlasting. Stacking and building with unit blocks the children exercise fine muscles, and explore, in a contest of good fun, some basic principles of geometry, math, and physics.

Cardboard blocks are inexpensive, and have the advantage of being lightweight and totally safe for smaller children. Even if a tall tower of cardboard blocks topples over, no harm can be done. These blocks, which can be purchased from any of the school supply stores such as Constructive Playthings, come flat and are to be assembled by the parents or teachers. They usually are covered with a brick-like appearance so that "houses" built with cardboard blocks are delightfully attractive.

Homemade blocks can be devised from plastic milk cartons, where the pouring end is cut off and a similar sized carton is fitted into the open end to make a hollow block with two solid ends. The cartons can be covered with contact paper for a more pleasing appearance. By making blocks from cartons of different sizes, variety is introduced into this "homemade" set.

We have explored here a few possibilities for setting the stage in which children can engage in informal exercise and play. The possibilities are unlimited in this area. We move on, now, to discuss another approach to physical development.

Formal Exercise

Coupled with the kind of free-form exercise described above, there should also be some directed activity for the physical development of children. Directed activity can be done with a total classroom of children, or with small groups taken apart from the other children. In this kind of learning experience, the children move at the suggestion of the adult leader. But even in this group setting there can be much room for individual expression. The children are not regimented, but guided, into meaningful uses of their bodies.

For instance the leader may suggest that the children stretch out their arms and pretend that they are airplanes with outstretched wings. The "airplanes" can then proceed to

coast around the room, "wings" still outstretched. Or the children can imagine that they are birds, flying or gliding through the air, and they can go through the whole-self motions of "winging" their way through the "wide sky." If music is played to accompany these motions, the experience is lifted to a heightened effect. The music could include symphonic "soaring" effects, or children's rhythm records.

At the beginning and the ending of each of these movement exercises, it is important for each child to have his or her own "space" from which to operate. So when the children have finished being birds, they are asked to fly back to their own spaces to rest. The activity has an underlying order to it, when each child knows where to return after "soaring in the clouds."

Emerging again from their own spaces, the children can try other body skills such as galloping like horses, crawling like caterpillars, or twirling like falling leaves. Imaginations are stimulated as bodies are put into full use in these simulation exercises.

Even more formal than the simulation experiences are the guided exercise times. For these periods, the children stand each in his own space, and follow the instructions such as, "Let's reach up high with our arms—high, high as if we are pushing the ceiling right up through the roof!" Or, "Now let's push our arms out to our sides, as far out as we can reach, as if we are pushing the walls farther and farther apart." Or "Now let's bend over and let our arms hang limp like rag dolls, and then reach way down to touch our toes with our fingers."

Sometimes these exercises can be set to song, such as the musical instructions to touch "heads and shoulders, knees and toes." Once the children learn a sequence, they can then elaborate upon it. For instance the teacher may suggest going through the touching of head, shoulders, knees, and toes very slowly, as in slow motion movies. After the slow motion, the group can then try fast motion, going through the touching sequence very rapidly, like a speeded-up record player. The children are thus getting not only exercise but also concept formation of the ideas of fast and slow!

Another method of guided exercise is the "problem-solving" approach. In this approach, the children as a group are presented with a challenge but are not given specific ways to meet it. For instance the teacher could ask the children how they could support their bodies off of the ground with only one support. To meet the challenge, one child might stand on one foot, while another might sit on his bottom with legs and arms in the air. Both children would have met the challenge, and the leader would happily acknowledge their success.

Then the teacher could ask for an example of supporting the body above the ground on two supports. This is, of course, the easiest challenge, because it can be met merely by standing on two feet. But the clever child will think up other ways, such as using one foot and one hand on the ground, with the rest of the body above. Another might sit and put one foot on the ground. All are correct as long as only two parts of the body touch the ground. Then the instructions could go on to suggest resting the body on three supports. It might be two legs and a hand, or it might be two hands and a foot. Four-year-olds go for this problem-solving approach because it gives them a challenge not only in body use but also in addition. The challenge could go on up to five supports, such as two hands, two feet, and a head!

Then there could be a new "wrinkle" to the problem-solving approach. The leader could pose the problem: "How many ways can we think of to get our bodies from one side of the room to the other?" The children are soon busy demonstrating these ways, which include hopping, jumping, skipping, walking, running, crawling, rolling, skooting, or wriggling. Children might take turns demonstrating their ways, so that the leader can write down and read back the many suggestions that have been explored for moving a body from one side of the room to the other. Then the problem-solving challenge could change. The teacher might pose the new problem: "How many ways can we find to move a chair from one side of the room to the other?" The children are then busily engaged in pushing the chair, pulling the chair, carrying the chair, rolling the chair, etc. Perhaps one child will think of bringing in another object such as a wagon for transporting the chair. In any event, the children are having fun, getting exercise, and developing thinking skills all in this one problem-solving project!

Other exercise games can involve the use of a rope. Children can play "tug of war" or can jump the rope or can make a rope circle on the floor. Then they can play jumping in and out of the rope circle. Or they can have several ropes and make several circles. They are then to do different motions in the different circles such as hopping in one, jumping in another, and crawling into the third. Where there are several different challenges such as this, we have a sequence activity that invites the children to remember the order of entering and exiting from each area.

Sequence activities are popular and nicely developmental. "Follow the Leader" is a time-honored sequence activity in which children follow and imitate the actions of the first child in the line. In the original game, the "leader" originates his or her own sequence. But then there can be an obstacle course set up by the teacher where the children all follow a prescribed routine. The advantage of the obstacle course is that it will be carefully planned to give a good variety of experiences. A good obstacle course will have something for the children to go over, something to go under, something to go around, something to go through, and items to go between. This kind of obstacle course teaches prepositional directions of "over, under, around, through, and between." It is important for children to learn to see themselves in relation to their environment, and to learn this kind of directionality in an atmosphere of games and fun.

A story will make the obstacle course even more exciting. For instance there is a book called *Bears in the Night* that tells of bears at home in bed hearing something sounding in the night. The bears get out of bed, go down the tree, over the bridge, under the log, around the lake, through the meadow until—"Whoo" they hear and see the owl. Then they reverse direction to go back through the meadow, around the lake, under the log, over the bridge, up the tree, and back to bed again. By the end of the event the children have enacted a story, have had experience in maneuvering their bodies in many positions, and have had one more experience in learning the concept of reversibility!

In addition to these activities, we can also plan for challenges by the use of masking tape on a bare floor. We can make a large square, at least five by five feet. The children are to lie

in the square and see if they can stretch their arms and legs out to touch each side. This may make a big stretch for some children but the challenge is to see how "big" they can make their bodies stretch.

We can then have a small square, no more than two feet across. The new challenge is to have the children curl up inside the square to see how small they can make their bodies. They may need to try several positions—such as the knee-chest position, to find the way to be "smallest." This is not a competitive game but a challenge for the child's own use of body movement.

A long straight line of masking tape on the floor can be used for "tightrope" walking. This exercise gives children the "heel-toe" practice, and can also be tried in reverse (walking backward on the line). Then a variation can be the walking astride the line, with one foot on each side. A more challenging variation is to have them walk astride the line with feet criss-crossing the line, with the left foot going to the right of the line and the right foot going to the left of the line, alternating in this kind of zig-zag manner.

Footprints from construction paper and taped to the floor are good for teaching left-right directionality. Place the foot prints, (cut to show obviously the form of a left and a right foot,) in a path that is comfortable for the children to walk. If the left foot prints are a different color from the right, the experience is highlighted. Then let the children call out "left," "right" as they step from footprint to footprint!

With imagination, a teacher can "rig" up many such adventures for small children. Challenges such as, "Can you find a partner and make a square of your two bodies together?" are for more advanced children. Or, "Can you make a triangle with two persons together?" Or, "Can you make a triangle of three persons together?" Or, "Can you make a rectangle of four persons together?" These more advanced exercises give practice in working together as well as solving challenges that involve whole bodies.

With rhythm instruments (which can be bought or homemade) the children can march to music and fee the lilting spirit of celebration. Or if it is time to have a more quiet experience, let the children sit on the rug and go through the motions of finger plays. Parents and teachers should have a repertoire of finger plays to do with small children. Such classics as "Where is Thumbkin" or "Open-shut them" or "Eency Teency spider" are always handy for group relaxation.

Fingerplays:

Where is Thumbkin?

(One thumb is held up, other hand behind back)
"Where is Thumbkin? Where is Thumbkin?"
(Other hand appears, with thumb up, fingers curled)
"Here I am, Here I am"
(First thumb asks)
"How are you today, sir?"
(Second thumb answers)
"Very well, I thank you"
(Both thumbs go behind back)
"Run away, Run away!"
(Index finger is held up, other hand behind back;
motions are the same as with the thumbs)
"Where is pointer? Where is pointer?"
"Here I am. Here I am"
"How are you today, sir?"
"Very well, I thank you."
"Run away. Run away!"
(Repeat these motions with third, then fourth, then fifth fingers, using the questions:)
"Where is tall man?" (third finger)
"Where is ring man?" (fourth finger)
"Where is pinky?" (fifth finger).

Eency teency spider went up a water spout;
Down came the rain and washed the spider out.
Out came the sun and dried up all the rain;
Eency teency spider went up the spout again.

Open, shut them, open shut them,
Give a little clap;
Open, shut them; open, shut them,
Put them in your lap.

Creep them, creep them,
Creep them, creep them,
Right up to your chin!
Open up your little mouth,
But do not put them in.

Group time can also be an occasion for "Going on a Bear Hunt" in which the leader gives out a phrase and a motion which the children mimic as the story progresses.

The Bear Hunt

Leader sits facing children as they sit cross-legged on a rug. Leader says each phrase, making hand motions to go with it; children echo each phrase and motion after the leader, as follows:

"We're going on a bear hunt" (pat hands alternately on knees to make a walking sound).
"We're walking through the woods" (more walking sounds).
"We come to a meadow" (stop walking sounds).
"We look out over the meadow" (hand to forehead as if looking far away).
"We go through the meadow—tall grass" (Hands make motions as if separating tall grass).

"We come to a lake, gotta swim it" (arms make swimming motion).
"We come to a mountain, gotta climb it" (Arms make motion of going up one side and down the other)

"WE SEE A BEAR!" Quick, run back home" (with each phrase repeat motions rapidly).

"Over the mountain."
"Swim the lake."
"Go through the meadow, tall grass."
"Go through the woods."
"We're home!"

The opportunities for group exercise activities are unlimited—but books in the bibliography can add to your own growing repertoire as a parent or as a teacher.

Occasionally children enjoy circle games such as "Duck, Duck Goose." For a game such as this, the children sit in a circle on the floor. One child becomes "it" and travels around the outside of the circle touching each child on the head and saying, "duck," for each person. Then without warning the child who is "it" will touch one child and instead of saying, "duck" will say, "goose." The child designated as "goose" must rise up and chase "it" around the circle to touch him or her. "It" runs around and sits down in the place of the child who was chosen "goose" so that "goose" now becomes the new "it" and the game continues.

This game can be mind-expanding if the designations are changed from time to time. For instance, instead of naming each child by one name, the person being "it" can name each child a different name within one category. If the category is fruit, "it" can say as he touches the children's heads, "apples," "pears," "oranges," "grapes"—and then name something that is not in the fruit category such as "hot dogs!" "Hot dogs" must jump up and run around the circle in the same way that "goose" did in the earlier version of the game. This form of the game requires the children to think about like objects in a category and to distinguish the word that does not fit. Many variations on this basic game can be fun and good for thinking and physical skills. The book

Teacher's Handbook of Children's Games, listed in the bibliography has many good games for physical development.

Then, of course, there are the time-honored physical activities centering around balls and bean bags. A simple game of tossing a large ball is a good beginning. To have the children in a circle and toss the ball to one child, calling that child by name, is a good "get acquainted" experience. That child can come into the center of the circle and call another child by name and toss the ball, and so on. Bean bags can be used in this way also. But with preschool children, it is important not to have games that involve competition. The goal is the fun of the activity, and the body-building exercise.

Wholesome Nutrition

Physical development involves not only exercise but also nutrition. Too often, children think of a snack as "something sweet." Our task as parent and teacher educators is to enable children to enjoy foods that are nutritious. Nursery schools usually begin in September for the school year. September is apple time. It can be exciting to go to an apple tree and gather the ripe fruit from the branches. Then when the apples are brought back to the home or classroom, the children are already interested in how they taste.

Apples can be served raw, whole or sliced. If sliced across, they will show the seed pattern that resembles a star. Other apples can be cooked into applesauce, or made into uncooked applesauce with the aid of a blender. Apples can also be made into tarts, pies, apple butter, or apple juice. It is exciting and nutritious to see how many ways we can enjoy this great fall fruit. Other fruits, too, can be "celebrated" in this kind of varied approach. Perhaps there are books that will carry out the apple theme into story time—books such as *Johnny Appleseed.*

Since children need the experience of spreading, good snacks can be made with crackers and peanut butter or crackers and cheese spread. Let the children spread their own crackers! If the food is interesting and filling, it is not necessary to have a sweet drink at each snack time.

Raw vegetables can be as exciting as raw fruit, if the children have had a chance to prepare them themselves. Children love to scrape carrots and cut celery stalks and pull apart the little "flowers" on a head of cauliflower. Books that show how things grow with roots, stems, and leaves can heighten the interest in vegetables. A trip to the grocery store to buy the raw vegetables is educational. Then at snack time, these raw treats can be served with a sour cream dip. If children, early in life, develop a taste for nutritional foods, instead of starchy foods, they may avoid the excessive weight problems that many members of our society today suffer. What can be more fun than cooking in the classroom? It is fascinating to children to measure, stir, and pour the ingredients for making bread. To see the dough go into the oven in a moist form and come out solid is truly a revelation of one of the wonders of life. Sometimes the children at Eden Laboratory School make bread sticks, so that each child can roll out his own dough and shape it individually. To eat one's own creation is a treat long to be remembered!

Finger jello can be made from the recipe on the unflavored gelatine box. and it is not only nutritional but educational. In a short period of time it changes from liquid to solid, so that it can be cut in squares and eaten like a little cake. Another adventure from liquid to solid is the making of butter. A small amount of whipping cream in a baby food jar can be shaken for about five minutes and will turn into butter. The children can then spread it on soda crackers and use it for a snack.

Part of a valid preschool curriculum should be the learning of the basic food groups. Children as young as three or four can identify foods as belonging to the "bread and cereal" group, or the "fruits and vegetables" group, or the "dairy products" group, or the "meats and fish" group. A game of "lotto" can be played with pictures from the various food groups. If children learn early in life the balanced dietary needs of the human body, they develop eating patterns that make for health and long life.

Day care centers can plan menus that exemplify the four food groups, and it is a good idea to let the children talk ahead of time about what to expect at the next meal. Children increase their appetites and interest in food in this kind of educational approach. Families, too, need to involve the children in an awareness of the foods served and reason for each. This is not to make a chore of eating, but to heighten the interest.

Along with knowing the food groups, the children also can benefit from a study of their own body parts. A simplified study of the human body, with the aid of visual resources such as McGraw Hill's *Moveable Melvin,* can help the child understand himself better, and take better care of his own body. It has been said that, "the body is the temple of the soul" and certainly it is a gift to be treasured.

We have explored together in this chapter three basic approaches to physical development: informal exercise, formal exercise, and wholesome nutrition. Growing bodies are wonders that unfold in a seemingly miraculous way, yet we as parents and teachers can enjoy the privilege of being a helpful part of the developing process.

Epilogue

We have been exploring together in these pages the many ways in which children grow and develop. We have explored some of the ways of intellectual development, social-emotional growth, spiritual growth, and physical development. Above all, we have noted that this optimum growth does not "just happen." It takes the sensitivity and skill of adult planners—parents and teachers—to organize the environment that nurtures children in their positive unfolding. This environment needs careful attention, so that all facets of development take place. Although we have studied these growth areas separately in each chapter, we know that in actuality, the child grows as a whole person, with the advances in the many areas happening simultaneously.

A model for whole growth is given in the scriptural passage of Luke: 2:52 where we read: "And Jesus increased in wisdom and in stature, and in favor with God and man." All four areas of increase which Jesus exemplified have become the areas of exploration which we have pursued in this volume. This kind of balanced growth makes for whole-ness of personhood, and is the goal of all human development.

As educators of small children, then, we are entrusted with the challenge of nurturing the little ones in this kind of well-rounded program. It is not enough to concentrate on only one facet of growth, when we have been given a whole child to guide and nurture. Our challenge is great, our privilege is overwhelming, our frustrations are inevitable, and our joys will be beyond number! The writer Kahil Gibran in his book *The Prophet* has these words of wisdom for all who work with small children:

"You are the bows from which
your children as living arrows
are sent forth.
The Archer sees his mark on the
pathway of the infinite, and He
bends you with his might that
His arrows may go swift and far.
Let your bending in the Archer's
hands be for gladness;
For as he loves the arrow that flies,
so
He loves also the bow that is stable."

Appendix

People of Other Lands—Preschool units

Unit I—Japan

From picture books taken from the library, show Japanese children, and Japanese homes.

At one table, try *origami* (paper folding). Special origami paper can be bought at Maruyama's at 18th and Chestnut, St. Louis, Mo., but if you cannot get that, use type-writer paper cut into perfect squares.

FOLD

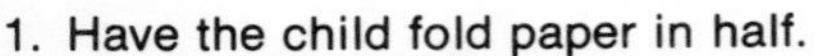

1. Have the child fold paper in half.
2. Have him fold again so that paper is a smaller square.
3. Have him open the smaller square so that the paper is in shape no. 1 (below), but the new crease shows. Then have him fold each outside edge to meet at the crease.

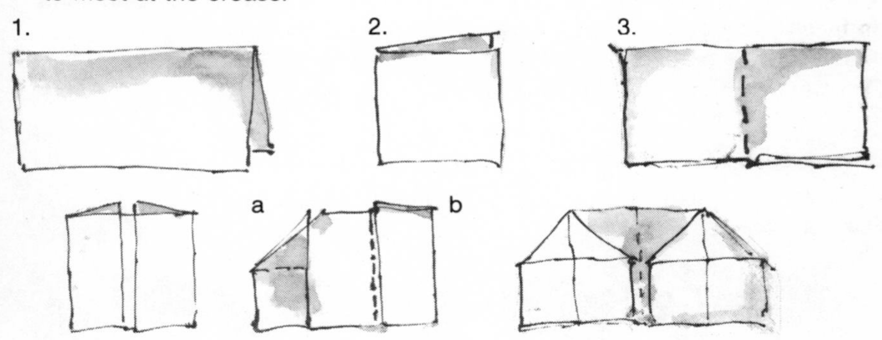

4. Have him lift the top paper from side (a) and revolve it out flat, running a finger up the inside crease of side (a) and pressing down the triangular "roof"

Repeat for side (b)

Let child draw windows and doors if he or she wants to.

Another group can make Japanese lanterns to string across the room for decorations. To make these, fold construction paper in half, cut parallel slits along the fold, and open out, and staple the top and bottom edges together.

(slits are perpendicular to fold)

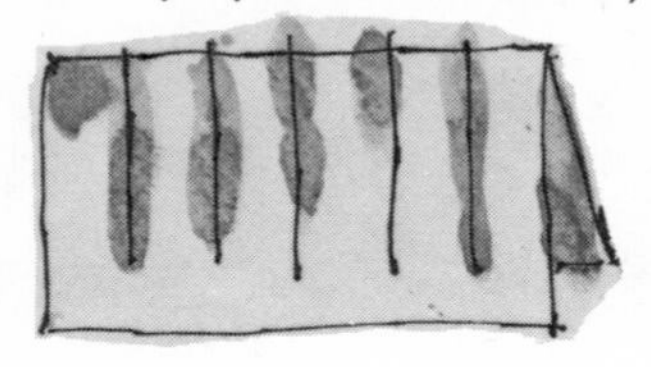

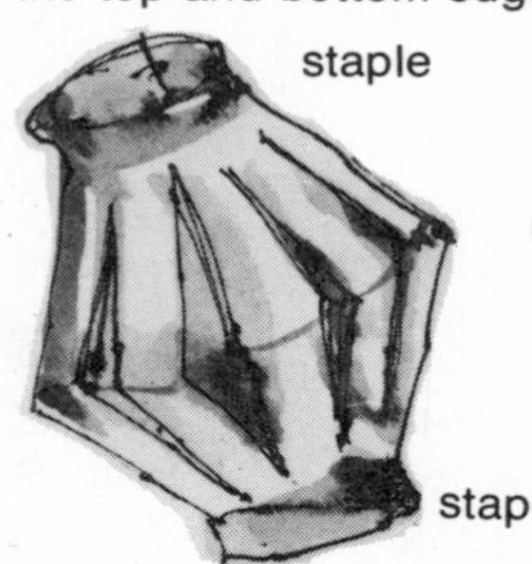

Cook Sukiyaki on an electric skillet in classroom. Let children help cut the vegetables. Recipe:

2 pounds steak cut in 1/4 inch cubes
mushrooms cut in tree shapes (1/2 lb)
celery cut diagonally—four stalks
scallions cut in 1 inch pieces (1 bunch)

1 lb fresh spinach, shredded
1/2 cup beef bouillon
1/2 cup soy sauce
3 tbs sugar

Brown steak in 4 tbs corn oil; add mixture of bouillon, soy sauce, and sugar; add celery and onions, for 3 minutes, add mushrooms and spinach for 3 more minutes, serve on rice.
(You can get chop sticks at Maruyama's and let them try eating with them.)

Have Japanese music playing in background—records from library—
Children can make "carp banners" (2 feet long, shaped like fish, colored brightly)

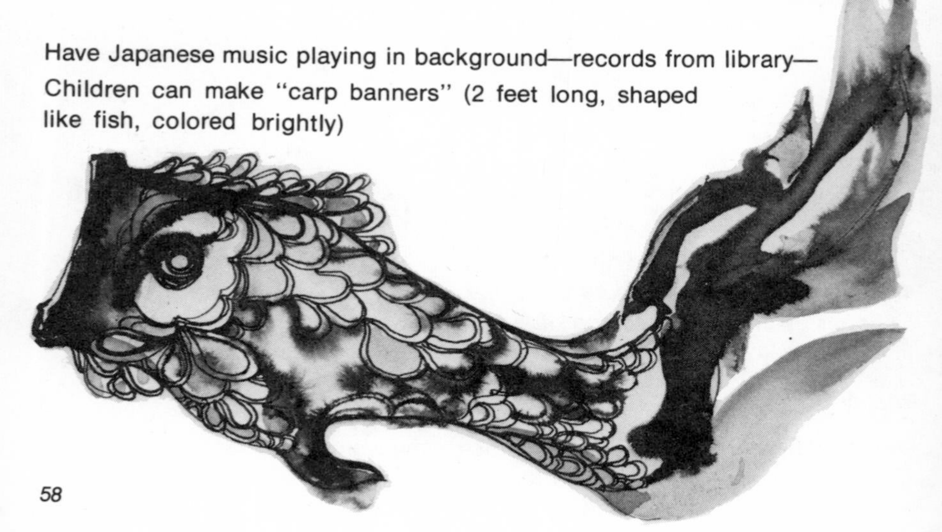

Unit 2—Mexico

Have pictures of Mexico and Mexican people around the room.

Have Mexican music playing on record player.

Let children make "serape" from brown wrapping paper, colored brightly with felt markers, and with edges fringed by scissors.

Enable children to make a "pinata" from paper mache over balloon. When this dries, they can paint it, and fill it with wrapped candies. Then it is tied to a limb or an overhanging joist and dangled on string. Children take turns with eyes closed "swatting at it" till it breaks and children scramble for candy. This is a favorite event at a Mexican celebration.

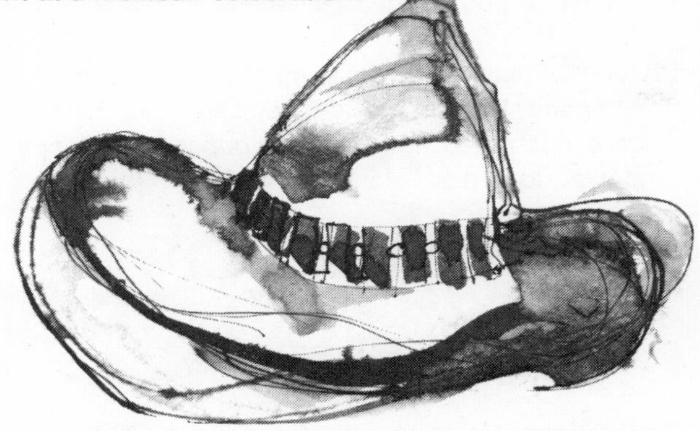

Let children dance to the music of the Mexican Hat Dance. They do not need to get the steps in precision order, but merely to keep the rhythm. If possible, have a sombrero in the center that they can dance around.

Bring in some Mexican clothing for children to see—hang them in the room. If the sizes are small enough, let the children try on the clothing.

Cut the easel paper in the shape of a Mexican Hat, and let the children paint it bright colors.

Let the children make items from clay and then paint when dry. The self-hardening white chalk clay in moist form can be ordered from Bradburn School Supply Store, 3118 Watson Rd., St. Louis, Mo.

Let the children help make Tacos to eat. You can buy the shells already made at grocery stores. In a skillet in the classroom, brown hamburger meat. Then have lettuce, tomatoes which the children have helped slice, and shredded cheese to go into the Taco shells.

Children will also enjoy making shakers to use as rhythm instruments to accompany Mexican music. They can make them from beans in orange juice cans, decorated, and also from popcorn (unpopped) in aluminum pie plates stapled together.

Gather books on Mexico from the library. There is a new and very nice one called: *The Christmas Pinata,* by Jack Kent, Parents' Magazine Press.

A film you can borrow from the library to show on Mexico is: "Mexican Boy, Story of Pablo"—Life in a Mexican Farm Village.

A filmstrip you can order is "If you Were Born in Mexico"—Constructive Playthings, 1040 East 85th St., Kansas City, Missouri 64131.

Ann Schroer et. al.
Eden Laboratory School

People of Other Lands—Preschool Units

Unit 3—Africa

Read stories of African folk tales with the children, picking colorful versions. *The Adventures of Spider* retold by Joyce Arkhurst, illustrated by Pinkney, can be bought paperback from Scholastic Press, 904 Sylvan Ave. Englewood Cliffs, N. J. 07632.

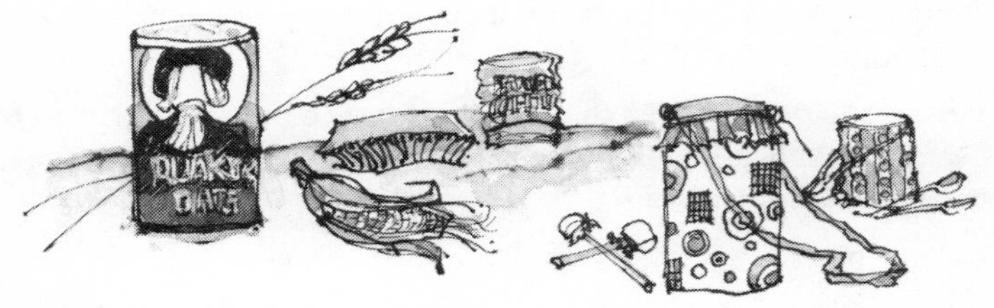

Play African music such as the record "Voices of Africa" Nonesuch Records, 15 Columbus Circle, New York City, 10023. Public libraries abound in African records and books. Folkways Scholastic Records on Africa can be ordered from Scholastic Press (address above).

Order *Fun and Festival from Africa* by Rose Wright from Wright Studio, 5264 Brookville Road, Indianapolis, Indiana 46219. Then let the children play some of the games such as "Takodi-Kodi," and cook some of the recipes.

Don't miss the fun of making "Peanut Soup."

This can be done over a stove, or in the classroom in a "crock pot," by the following recipe:

One 6 oz. jar of peanut butter, chunky.

Four cups of chicken bouillon. (or two cups bouillon and two cups water)

One onion, chopped.

One tomato, chopped.

Combine all ingredients and simmer for 1/2 hour.

(There are other recipes for peanut soup, using real chicken and real peanuts, and one can improvise to taste.)

Another treat is banana cut in inch segments and rolled in grated coconut.

And what shall the child wear to the African gathering? Try making dashikis with the children. These can be made from a square piece of white sheet material, (four feet square, or smaller, with a hole in the center for the child's head). Decorate the material with bright colors, printed onto the cloth by the children. This can be done by using textile paint, or tempora paint, and print shapes such as sponge shapes or empty spools. The child dips the shape into the paint and prints it on to the cloth, using different colors to make the garment beautifully colorful.

Paper bag masks can be fun to make, and colorful. The bags (about the size of a child's head) can be cut with holes for eyes and mouth and then painted as colorfully as the child desires.

Rhythm instruments can be made from oatmeal boxes (for drums) and other items such as coffee cans.

Be sure to invite a visitor who has been to Africa, if possible.

Other resources:

The Beauty of Being Black, by Olivia Pearl Stokes. Friendship Press, 475 Riverside Drive, New York City.

Filmstrip: "African A.B.C." Constructive Playthings, 1040 East 85th St. Kansas City, Missouri 64131.

Love One Another, illustrated by Marcel Nday, translated by Robert Koenig, Philadelphia, United Church Press (1505 Race Street).

Cut Outs of Africans, Africa Poster, Africa Madonna Print, African Masks Favors, and other similar items can be ordered from Wright Studio, address above.

Bibliography

Bibliography for teacher enrichment

Association for Childhood Education International, *Physical Education for Children's Healthful Living.* 6315 Wisconsin Ave. N.W. Washington, D.C.

Bainton, Roland, *Church of our Fathers.* Philadelphia: Westminster Press, 1950.

Baratta-Lorton, Mary, *Workjobs.* Menlo Park, Calif.: Addison-Wesley, 1972.

Berends, Polly B., *Whole Child, Whole Parent.* New York: Harper's Magazine Press, 1975.

Buber, Martin, *I and Thou.* New York: Charles Scribner's Sons, 1937.

Carson, Rachel, *The Sense of Wonder.* New York: Harper and Row, 1956.

Cherry, Clare, *Creative Movement for the Developing Child.* Belmont, Calif, Fearon, 1968. *Creative Art for the Developing Child.* Belmont, Calif, Fearon, 1972.

Dixon, Dorothy, *Growth in Love.* West Mystic, Conn.: Twenty-Third Publications, 1972.

Duska, R. and Whelan, M., *Moral Development, A Guide to Piaget and Kohlberg.* New York: Paulist Press, 1975.

Erickson, Eric, *Childhood and Society:* New York: W.W. Norton and Co. 1950.

Fraiberg, Selma, *The Magic Years.* New York: Charles Scribner's Sons, 1959.

Fowler, James, "Toward a Developmental Perspective on Faith." *Religious Education* March-April, 1974.

Furth, Hans, *Piaget for Teachers.* Englewood Cliffs, N.J.: Prentice-Hall, 1970. *Thinking Goes to School,* New York: Oxford University Press, 1974.

Goldman, Ronald, *Readiness for Religion.* New York: Seabury Press, 1970.

Hendrick, Joanne, *The Whole Child.* St. Louis: C.V. Mosby Company, 1975.

Heschel, Abraham J., *Between God and Man.* New York: Harper and Row, 1959.

Ilg, F. and Amew, L., *Child Behavior.* New York: Harper and Brothers, 1955.

Keen, Sam, *Apology for Wonder.* New York: Harper and Row, 1969.

McMahon, E. M. and Campbell, P., *Please Touch.* New York: Sheed and Ward, 1969.

Moran, Gabriel, *Design for Religion.* New York: Herder and Herder, 1971.

Phillips, J. L., *The Origins of the Intellect, Piaget's Theory.* San Francisco: W. H. Freedman Co., 1969.

Sharp, Evelyn, *Thinking is Child's Play.* New York: Avon Books, 1971.

Standing, E.M., *Maria Montessori, Her Life and Work.* Fresno, Calif. Academy Library Guild, 1957.

Taylor, Margaret Fisk, *Time for Wonder.* Philadelphia: Christian Education Press, 1961.

Wadsworth, Barry, *Piaget's Theory of Cognitive Development.*

Westerhoff, J. and Neville, G., Generation to Generation. Richmond: John Knox Press.

Wirth, Marian, *Teacher's Handbook of Children's Games.* West Nyack, N.Y.: Parker Pub., 1976.

Yamamoto, Kaoru, *The Child and His Image.* Boston: Houghton-Mifflin, 1972.

Bibliography for use with children

Books:

Bemelmans, Ludwig, *Madeline.* New York: Viking Seafarer. 1939.

Cohen, Miriam, *Will I Have a Friend?* New York: Collier Books, 1967.

Eckblad, Edith, *Soft as the Wind.* Minneapolis: Augsburg Publishing House.

Freed, Alvin, *T.A. for Tots.* Sacramento, California: Jalmar Press, 1973.

Freeman, Don, *Corduroy.* New York: Viking Seafarer, 1968. *Dandelion.* New York: Viking Seafarer, 1964.

Goddard, Carrie, *Isn't it a Wonder?* Nashville: Abingdon Press, 1976.

Heide, Florence P., *God and Me.* St. Louis: Concordia Publishing House, 1975.

Keats, Ezra Jack, *The Snowy Day.* New York: Viking Press, 1962. *Whistle for Willie.* New York: Viking Seafarer, 1964.

Klein, Norma, *A Train for Jane.* Old Westbury, N.Y.: Femenist Press, 1974.

Muller, Edna C., *God Planned it That Way.* Nashville: Abingdon Press, 1952.

Roorbach, H. A., *I Learn About Sharing.* Nashville: Abingdon Press, 1968.

Thomas, Edith L. *The Whole World Singing.* New York: Friendship Press, 1950. (song book)

Woolcott, Carolyn, *I Can Talk with God.* Nashville: Abingdon Press, 1952. *I Can See What God Does.* Nashville: Abingdon Press, 1969.

Watson, Jane, and Switzer, R. E. *Sometimes I Get Angry.* New York: Golden Press, 1971. *Sometimes I'm Afraid.* New York: Golden Press, 1971.

Zolotow, Charlotte, *William's Doll.* New York: Harper and Row, 1972.

(Note: Many other titles of quality children's books can be found in: *Bibliography, Books for Children.* Association for Childhood Education International, 3615 Wisconsin Avenue, N. W. Washington, D.C. 20016. Also in catalogue for Scholastic paperbacks, 904 Sylvan Avenue, Englewood Cliffs, N.J.)

Multi-media kits:

American Guidance Service, Circle Pines, Minn.: "Developing Understanding of Self and Others."

Guidance Associates: Pleasantville, N.Y.: "A Strategy for Teaching Values"

Records:

Comea, Bill, "Busy Day for Children." N.Y.: Avante Garde Records (250 W. 57th St.).

Cone, Jane, "Adventures in Resting." New York, Decca Records, Inc.

Disney, Walt, Presents: "Let's Have a Parade." Favorite Marches for Children. Disneyland Record, 1964.

"Do, re mi and the songs Children Love to Sing." New York: Kapp Records.

International Children's Choir, "Take a Moment and Sing Along." Long Beach, California: Wide World Records (P.O. Box 5656 90805).

Ives, Burl, "Little White Duck, and other Favorites." New York: Harmony, product of Columbia Records (51 W. 52nd St.)

Jaye, Mary T., *Making Music Your Own.* Morristown, N.Y.: Silver Burdette. 1966.

Jenkins, Ella, "Adventures in Rhythm." Englewood Cliffs, N.J.: Scholastic Records. "And One and Two," New York: Folk Records (43 W. 61st St. 10023).

"Kindergarten Songs, Games, and Rhythms." Philadelphia: United Church Press, 1965.

McCormack, Marie, "Songs and Games of Physical Fitness." New York: Golden Records, (250 W. 57th St.).

Misterogers, "Won't You be my Neighbor?" Latrobe, Pa.: Small World Records "Let's Be Together Today." Small World Records,761 Two Gateway Center, Pittsburgh, Pa. 15222.

Palmer, Hap, "Getting to Know Myself." Freeport, N.Y.: Educational Activities, Inc., 1972. "Ideas,Thoughts and Feelings." Freeport, N.Y.: Educational Activities, 1973. "Learning Basic Skills Through Music" Educational Activities, 1969. "Modern Tunes for Rhythms and Instruments." Educational Activities, 1970.

"Sesame Street Book and Record Album." New York: Warner Brothers Records. (44 E. 50th).

"Sesame Street Record." New York: CBS, Inc. (51 W. 52nd St.).

Wise, Joe, "Close your Eyes, I got a Surprise." Phoenix, Ariz., North American Liturgy Resources, (2110 W. Peoria Ave. 85029).

Wood, Lucille, "December Holidays." Glendale, California: Bowmar, (622 Rodier St. 91201—this is one in a series of songs for each month).